Praise from authors and publishers for
Lissa Warren and *The Savvy Author's Guide to Book Publicity*

"In twenty years of dealing with publishers and publicists, Lissa Warren is without a doubt the most responsive, hardest-working, smartest, and most congenial publicist I have had the pleasure to work with. As for her new book on how authors can get publicity for their books, I give her six stars out of five."

—Howard Rheingold, author of the
national bestseller *Smart Mobs: The Next Social Revolution*

"There are few people who can make books really happen. Lissa Warren is one of them. Her book tells you how. Read it carefully. The advice is outstanding."

—Susan Rabiner, co-author of *Thinking Like Your Editor*
and co-owner of the Susan Rabiner Literary Agency

"Lissa Warren is the publicist's publicist. She is the consummate professional, the secret weapon in a publisher's arsenal of marketing tools."

—David Goehring, Director, Harvard Business School Press

"Any author who gets Lissa Warren as their publicist is very lucky indeed. She has an incredible energy level. She builds the book steadily from a base which expands gradually to a larger and larger audience, and most important, she stays with the book for months. Lissa has an exuberance, intelligence and deep bench of contacts that is wonderful for writers who have put a lot of time into their work."

—Bill Wolman and Anne Colamosca, authors of *The Great 401(k) Hoax*

"From an author's point of view, Lissa Warren is a dream to work with. I felt that she presented my book to the public effectively and ~~~~~tly for what it is. In fact, she helped m   Lissa

D1056162

knows every facet of the industry and provides level-headed advice while remaining imaginative in her approach. With Lissa you see what happens when enthusiasm meets reality: you get results."

—David Weinberger, co-author of the national bestseller *The Cluetrain Manifesto* and author of *Small Pieces Loosely Joined: A Unified Theory of the Web*

"A typical author's greatest fear is no one will hear of his book. With Lissa Warren as my publicist, my greatest fear has been that I will not show up at the right place, at the right time, because I can't keep all my public appearances straight—radio, television, newspapers, and magazines, local, national, and international. But she makes sure I do that, too. I began to think I had a right to appear in the *New York Times, Washington Post, Time* magazine, ABC News, and CNN."

—Steven Wise, author of *Drawing the Line: Science and the Case for Animal Rights* and *Rattling the Cage: Toward Legal Rights for Animals*

The Savvy Author's
Guide to
Book
Publicity

A Comprehensive Resource –
From Building the Buzz
to Pitching the Press

Lissa Warren

CARROLL & GRAF PUBLISHERS
NEW YORK

"Some reviews give pain. This is regrettable, but no author has any right to whine. He is not obliged to be an author. He invited publicity, and he must take the publicity that comes along."—E.M. Forster

THE SAVVY AUTHOR'S GUIDE TO BOOK PUBLICITY

Carroll & Graf Publishers
An Imprint of Avalon Publishing Group Incorporated
245 West 17th Street · 11th Floor
New York, NY 10011

Library of Congress Cataloging-in-Publication Data is available.

ISBN: 0-7867-1275-9

Interior design by Simon M. Sullivan
Printed in the United States of America
Distributed by Publishers Group West

Table of Contents

Introduction

Jonathan Lowenstein feared he had written a dud. Three weeks after its pub date, the book he'd spent four years researching—and two years writing—had a sales rank of 654,287 on Amazon.com. Only one customer review had been posted, and it gave the book one star out of five—enough to give it an overall rating of . . . one star. The masochist in him had developed a habit of checking the site each hour. And to make matters worse, his publicist, Jane, wasn't returning his calls.

Only weeks earlier, he'd been celebrating his book's advance reviews. Jane, who worked at the press that had published the book, had managed to get coverage in all four pre-publication magazines, and even the notoriously cranky *Kirkus Reviews* had called it "a tome worth reading." *Publishers Weekly*—or "*PW*" as it's known in the trade—had given it a star and included a shot of the cover. But so far he'd done only two interviews—and both of them were local. He wanted something national; he wanted National Public Radio. Ever since he'd started writing the book, he'd imagined Terry Gross, host of their popular *Fresh Air* show, saying "So tell me, Jon, how *does* a scientist come to write such lovely prose?"

His editor had said that bookstores had placed advance orders for more than twenty thousand copies—but it wasn't selling at Borders, and his Barnes & Noble numbers were down. His dream of a fat royalty check that would pay for his daughter's college had evaporated into the very air on which his book was based. It was called *The Smoke of Heaven* and it focused on pollution—how the worst affects of smog can be reversed for good. In his heart, Jonathan still believed in his book, but his head was saying "lemon."

Earlier that week, Jonathan had decided something needed to be done . . . and fast. He'd heard that every book has a very small window in which it needs to "pop," and that those that don't will be returned to the publisher's warehouse in truly frightful numbers. He sought advice from his writer friends, and one suggested hiring a freelance publicist whom she'd heard was very good. Jonathan called the freelancer and they had a promising talk. She assured him his book could "get media" and they even discussed the "hooks"—things that made the book unique and tied to current events. It was odd—and not a little humbling—to hear her boil his three-hundred-page book down to a ten-second pitch, but she was confident she could get reviews and off-the-book-page coverage. She emailed a formal proposal to him, and when it arrived he felt hope return and asked her to send a contract. She overnighted it to him, and he signed it and Fed Exed it back.

The next day he called Jane, but again he got her voicemail. He left a message giving the name of the freelance publicist he'd hired, asking Jane to contact her and send copies of his book. Not five minutes later his telephone rang, and a clearly ticked-off Jane was demanding to know why he'd "gone behind her back" and hired a freelance publicist. Jonathan was dumbfounded. Jane had never seemed that excited about the book, and he knew she had lots of others to handle. He'd expected her to be grateful—or, if nothing else, relieved.

It wasn't the first time he'd made her mad. A week ago, his book was reviewed in the prestigious journal *Nature*. They'd hated it, and had taken him to task on several points, bemoaning both his thesis and his "choppy" writing style. To make matters worse, he knew the reviewer—a former colleague whom he'd beaten out for a grant. In a fit of rage he'd banged out a letter to the editor, berating the journal for failing to screen reviewers for a "grudge." The magazine printed the letter, and when Jane stumbled upon it she e-mailed him to say:

> Jonathan,
> I was very surprised to see your letter in this week's issue of *Nature*. Had you consulted me, frankly, I'd have said don't write the thing. Authors always sound like they're whining in these notes. The exception is when they right factual wrongs, which you simply did not do. Instead, you were defensive, and I don't think it will help you. Next time, please involve me. I'm here to guide this book.
> Jane

He wrote her back and apologized for not keeping her in the loop, but said he didn't regret the letter or its slightly scathing tone. She replied that she thought a truce was in order. He wasn't sure if she was referring to a truce between them or a truce with *Nature*, but by then he'd tired of both the fights and simply hit "delete." Less than a minute later, he was checking his Amazon ranking again.

THE REALITIES OF BOOK PUBLICITY

Jonathan's situation is not unique. Almost all authors go through a period of intense nervousness when their books hit the stores, and they often feel the need to take publicity matters into their own hands.

Sometimes publishers jumpstart sales by running launch ads in prominent places like the *New York Times*, the *Wall Street Journal*, or *USA Today*. But at $30,000 per quarter-page, it's not something all houses can afford—at least, not for every book. Some books are bolstered early on by direct mail or online marketing campaigns, but they're not cheap either, and their results are hard to quantify.

More often than not, publishers rely on publicity to drive sales of the books they publish. They need their authors on radio and TV shows—preferably national ones. They need their authors profiled in high-circulation newspapers and glossy magazines, and they need the books reviewed there, too. Like publishers, authors crave this publicity, not only because they, too, want a bestseller, but because they've worked hard and alone for a long, long time, and feel they deserve their fifteen minutes. They're right; they do.

Enter "The Publicist," the person on whose shoulders the success of most books rides once they're done being edited. She (for some reason, it's almost always a she) is responsible for securing coverage of the book in as many print and broadcast media outlets as possible in the hope that it will cause customers to beeline it for the nearest bookstore. She aims high (think the *Today Show*) but often has to settle for smaller venues (think Connecticut Cablevision). She tries to time the coverage—national and local—so that it occurs right as books hit stores, when they're plentifully stocked and well-displayed. She's the one who writes your press release. She's the one who is always on the phone. She's the one whose voice mail chimes "you have twelve new messages" when she gets back from a half-hour meeting. She's the one with the precarious bookshelves, the one whose e-mail "sent" box numbers in the thousands even though the server wiped it clean just last month, the one who arranges for you to speak in bookstores, and the one who handles all of the details of your seven-city tour. If she's doing it right, her job is never done. If she's doing it wrong, your book is.

Most authors enter into the publicity process ready to help their publicist however they can. Often, they are able to see their book's strengths and potential media audience more clearly than the publicist, who may not be familiar with the fields relevant to the book's topic. Some authors are able to provide their publicist with the names of specific producers, reporters, and editors with whom they've had previous contact. Others can suggest shows and publications that may be appropriate for their book. But few authors have mastered the art of working with their publicist, and to be sure there are those who have mastered the art of working against her.

An average mid-sized publishing house puts out seventy-five to one hundred titles per year. They usually have a three- to four-person publicity department. That means in any given month a publicist is handling at least two new books while wrapping up the books that pubbed in the previous two or three months *and* laying the groundwork for the ones that will be coming out in the few months to come. Realistically, all you can hope for is a publicist who will create decent press material, pull adequate media lists, and do the mailings promptly.

So the finished book mailing goes out to the media. You brace yourself and wait. A week goes by, then two weeks. Another week. Still nothing. Does it mean your book is bad? Are your words and thoughts unworthy of the media's attention? Of course not. But you've got some work to do. The reality is that most publicity is generated by follow-up with the media, not by initial mailings. And most publicists have very little time to follow up. This means you need to get the media to go to your publicist, or somehow convince your publicist to push for a bit more press. Option three is to outsource—that is if you've got the bucks. Regardless of which path you choose, the rest is up to you. If you've written a book, you have a new job . . . and the name of that job is "publicist."

YOUR NEW JOB TITLE—"PUBLICIST"

Maybe you self-published it. Maybe you published it with a small press or a university press. Maybe you even published it with Random House or Knopf. No matter whom your publisher, no matter whether it's a novel, a biography, a collection of poetry, or a self-help book, when your book comes off press you want and need to know what happens next. What's more, you want to know what happens if nothing happens. And the sad truth is, more often than not, nothing does happen.

Over the course of a book's publishing life, most authors figure out what it actually takes to make it sell. Unfortunately, by then, it's often too late. There are myriad sales-boosting opportunities that exist for authors, and if you know ahead of time what to push for and what you yourself can do, your book can exceed your expectations. Without a doubt, as an author you need to know how to navigate the waters of book P.R., not just to maintain your sanity and calm your nerves, but because you're your book's most important asset.

I do stop short of advising authors to approach the media on their own behalf. Such attempts are rarely successful. Between their own brain-power and that of publicists, the media has enough ideas—more than they have time to run with, more than their pages or airtime could possibly ever hold. They have to draw the line somewhere, and they often draw it at authors because, let's face it, you're not exactly unbiased when it comes to your own book. What's more, since knowing the media's lingo and understanding its needs is not your full-time job, most editors, and reporters, and producers prefer to deal with publicists—with people whose *profession* it is to promote your book. Yes, publicists annoy them, too, from time to time—but at least they speak their language. Pursuing the press on your own behalf can create a bad reputation, and it can become quite demoralizing for you. But there's a ton of behind-the-scenes work that authors can do—work that will help your publicist help you; work that will definitely help your book.

If you do decide to pitch the media directly about your book, I advocate that you approach with tact and creativity, with finesse and common courtesy, and, of course, a solid pitch—for this is the kind of effort that truly gets results. I encourage you to see yourself as an "idea broker." You should have a "matchmaking" mentality as you seek to marry your knowledge and your book's information to the media's needs. True, you're doing the media a favor by providing them with the talking head they need to round out their TV segment, the voice they need to fill an hour of radio air time, the book review they need to fill a page of their magazine, or the quotes they need to flesh out their newspaper article. But they're doing you a favor, too. They are choosing you and your book over others. They are giving you attention that will get you attention. They are causing the consumer to seek out your book. So if you choose to go down this radical path, do so with a slice of humble pie—and the knowledge that it won't be easy going.

HOW *THE SAVVY AUTHOR'S GUIDE TO BOOK PUBLICITY* CAME TO BE

In my years in the publicity departments of four trade presses—David R. Godine, Houghton Mifflin, Perseus Publishing, and now Da Capo Press—and via a brief stint as a freelance literary publicist, I've become acutely aware of the ways in which authors can help, and hinder, their publicists. As a writer myself, I realize that their efforts are almost always well intentioned; they just want their book to get noticed and sell. I also realize that the mistakes authors make are often the result of poor communication on the part of the publicists—ironic for people whose communication skills supposedly landed them the job in the first place.

But I can't fault the publicists too much. They are, after all, a very busy lot. It's not unusual for in-house publicists to handle a dozen titles per "list" (a term that refers to each season or catalogue). They cannot give equal attention to each, and are, in fact, required not to do so. They're told to work hardest on books that advanced well (in other words, books that most bookstores have ordered—in very healthy numbers, no less), to take care of house authors, to recall what was paid up-front for each book (yes, your royalty advance really does make a difference). They cannot take time to explain the whole process—they cannot be teacher and publicist both.

The Savvy Author's Guide to Book Publicity grew out of the realization that I was being asked to explain the same things each time I started working with a new author. I saw that many first-time authors and even some seasoned authors have never had the publicity process adequately explained to them, and therefore don't know 1) how to help their publicist achieve good results for their book, or 2) what constitutes "good results" for their book. *The Savvy Author's Guide to Book Publicity* also has its roots in the fact that as a book publicist who happens to hold an MFA in Creative Writing, I'm constantly queried by writer friends who are frustrated with the lukewarm (or total lack of) effort put forth by their in-house publicists. They often feel the need to take at least partial ownership of what is happening to their book, but rarely do they know where to start. Furthermore, they don't realize that this feeling is normal—and, more often than not, warranted. The truth is, not every publicist can or will work hard on every book, and it doesn't mean the book is bad or lacks significant potential. *The Savvy Author's Guide to Book Publicity* is also the result of a panel I spoke on for PMA (Publishers Marketing Association) at the bookselling industry's annual convention, Book Expo America. In attendance were almost a hundred self-published or small press authors. They were smart and fun and funny, but their need for a one-stop, soup-to-nuts guide to book publicity was vividly apparent. They were "people without publicists," and their questions showed frustration—the kind that comes from making gaffs you didn't have to make; the kind that comes from being ignored, passed around, and lied to by bookstores and the media . . . and the publisher's staff.

THE GOALS OF *THE SAVVY*
AUTHOR'S GUIDE TO BOOK PUBLICITY

The Savvy Author's Guide to Book Publicity shows you how to evaluate and capitalize on your book's potential for media coverage and for events that lead to sales—in the short-term and the long-run. It shows you how to work with your publicist to get the word out about your book and also explains how to take matters into your own hands when you don't have a publicist or when your publicist isn't getting results—or even trying to. Each chapter contains practical information that will help you understand the lion's share of what happens to your book once it's off press, and how you can be helpful in the promotion process—or even spearhead it if you have to—so that your book receives maximum exposure on the radio, on TV, in magazines, in newspapers, and on the Web, as well as in bookstores. The advice is complemented by stories of your fellow authors—from the savvy to the shy, from the stoic to the scared—with tales of tours gone awry, bestsellers made and almost-made, and great and not-so-great author/publicist collaboration. It covers everything from creating your own press material, to targeting the right shows and publications, to pitching the media, to hiring people who can help you get the word out about your book. It even shows you how to secure bookstore events and other speaking engagements, as well as how to make them a success. So that you can become familiar with the various types of press material you can create (or help your publicist create), there's an appendix with sample galley letters, press releases, Q&As, talking points sheets, quizzes, and author bios. In addition, *The Savvy Author's Guide to Book Publicity* contains sample tour itineraries in the hope you'll want to travel to spread the word about your book. And, finally, there's an index for quick reference to a wealth of information that will help you sell your book.

The Savvy Author's Guide to Book Publicity shows you why you need to be actively involved in the promotional process for your book, and how you can be the best advocate for it—with your publisher's sales force, with booksellers, directly with potential readers, and, if absolutely necessary, with the media. It educates you about the book promotion process and how you can work with a publicist (either in-house or freelance) and other marketing and communications specialists to get your book the exposure that will help it reach—or even exceed—its sales potential. It provides you with the opportunity to understand book publicity the way publishers do—what it can and can't do for a book, and how it can do different things for different kinds of books. And, if you're a self-published author or an author who has published with a very small press, it teaches you how to navigate the waters of book P.R. alone . . . and to do so successfully.

The Savvy Author's Guide to Book Publicity is built on the philosophy that it is possible to get attention for your book without resorting to shameless self-promotion. Throughout, it demonstrates fine touches and advocates decorum, which always get you further than pushiness or hype. As someone actually employed at a publishing house—an industry insider, a "publishing professional"—it's my hope that I can provide the kind of insight that you can't get from your fellow authors or from general P.R. consultants. *The Savvy Author's Guide to Book Publicity* is intended for any kind of author and any kind of book. I've built bestsellers, but also worked successfully on books that could never be bestsellers. I've handled books that are very literary as well as books that are more commercial.

Keep in mind that any effort to get maximum exposure will leave you feeling maximally exposed. The merits of your book will be publicly debated. At times it will feel personal; at times it may be so. But in the end you'll have a clearer sense of what your book's about, of what you have to offer, of what you've really done. And hopefully, you'll have a book that's sold and that will sell long after all the interviews and autographs are done.

Chapter 1

What Is Book Publicity?

You spend months—maybe years—writing your book. It's edited, copy-edited, and proofread. The cover is designed. The font is selected and the pages are laid out. It goes to press where it's printed and then bound. It ships to the publisher's distributor, who ships it to the stores. The next step is to get the customer to go to the store and buy it. There are a number of ways to accomplish this, but for many books, the best is through publicity.

WHAT IS BOOK PUBLICITY?

In a nutshell, book publicity is print and broadcast coverage of your book. It can take many forms.

Print coverage generally includes newspapers, magazines, newsletters, wire services (Associated Press, Bloomberg News, Dow Jones News, Reuters, Scripps Howard, United Press International, etc.), and Web sites. It may mean reviews, Q&As (question and answers—sort of a transcript of an interview with you, though it's generally edited rather than printed verbatim), excerpts (when a portion of your text is reproduced, sometimes exactly as it appears in your book and other times with tweaking that you'll have to help out with), profile pieces (articles that focus on you but also mention your book), feature articles (which focus on an issue, but quote you as an expert and mention your book by identifying you as "author of"), online chats (live interaction between you and the public where they ask you questions and you supply the answers either by typing them yourself or giving them to a transcriber by phone), or online message boards (which you moderate by logging on at your convenience).

Broadcast coverage generally refers to radio and TV. Sometimes it's an interview specifically about your book. Other times you're a talking head, speaking about an issue that somehow relates to your book. In both instances, your book gets plugged. When it's a TV interview, they may even flash the book cover on-screen or chyron you as "author of" (a chyron is the identifying text that appears briefly beneath you as you're talking).

WHY IS IT IMPORTANT?

A wide variety of books become bestsellers—everything from *Chicken Soup for the Soul*, to hefty biographies, to thrillers, to literary novels. What most have in common is strong publicity. It's the main thing that drives consumers into the bookstores and appears more trustworthy than advertising because it contains the judgment of an independent third party. Each new book is competing for the customer's attention—and the customer's dollar—against recent but well-established titles and also the classics. And new books compete with each other. According to R. R. Bowker's *Books In Print*, more than 150,000 books were published in 2002—a six percent jump from the previous year, and the number has been rising since 1999. More than 17,000 of those titles were fiction (making it the largest, and therefore most competitive category) and over 10,000 of them were books for children or young adults.

Apart from the consumer marketplace, it's also important to understand that publicity holds a crucial place in the publishing process. The marketing, subrights, and sales departments all key off of publicity. Good publicity—and lots of it—provides them with the ammunition they need to successfully do their jobs. It enables them to create better ads and secure more course-adoptions. It helps them get more interest and money from paperback houses and presses overseas. It results in more and bigger buys from chain bookstores like Barnes & Noble, Walden, and Borders, and wholesalers like Baker & Taylor and Ingram. In short, it's truly critical to any book's overall success.

All of this is a way of saying that you want your book to get wide coverage. That said, some books are "publicity-driven" while other books are not.

THE "PUBLICITY-DRIVEN" BOOK

If your book is more of a word-of-mouth or marketing-dependent book, it's important to focus your efforts accordingly. So how can you tell?

Generally speaking, fiction, poetry, and memoirs are rather word-of-mouth driven. They sell because friends recommend them to each other. A few good examples are *The Lovely Bones* by Alice Sebold, the poetry of Mary Oliver (who refuses to even grant interviews), and Dave Eggers's book about raising his brother, *A Heartbreaking Work of Staggering Genius*. Publicity can help you get the word-of-mouth going for these kinds of books, but it's mostly a means to an end. Readings at bookstores also help generate word-of-mouth, and while these readings are often lumped into a book's publicity campaign (and arranged by the publicist), it doesn't mean the book is truly a publicity-driven one. The best way to generate word-of-mouth: write a damn fine book.

Certain kinds of nonfiction are very publicity-driven. Biographies fall into this category. So do books on business, science, and politics, and also current affairs. If they're not covered by the press, most people will not hear about them. And that means they won't buy them. Some other kinds of nonfiction books tend to benefit from publicity, though their success depends more on tapping into large core interest groups. This is true for cookbooks, for example, where the vibrant "foodie" community embraces titles on a regular basis. Same for photography books.

Books that fall into the reference category—including titles on parenting and health, and things like travel guides—tend to be much more marketing-dependent than publicity-driven. They'll sell if people receive brochures about them or see them advertised in places they always turn to for advice. These are books that need to be well-stocked and displayed in stores, since people who shop for these kinds of books often select from what's in front of them. The *Savvy Author's Guide to Book Publicity* falls into this category. It will only appeal to a small segment of the population, and therefore won't benefit all that much from mass media (and won't likely receive it). My time will be best spent on grassroots marketing efforts to get the word out directly to the folks who need it.

PUBLICITY TRENDS

Every kind of publicity has its trends. Lately, for television, the rise of the evening newsmagazine (*20/20*, *Dateline*, *48 Hours*, *Primetime*, *60 Minutes*, and *60 Minutes* II) has been noticeable, as has the proliferation of on-air book clubs (*Oprah* and *Regis and Kelly*—even the *Today Show*). This means more opportunities for author coverage. But there's also pressure on the morning shows to "get The Get" (meaning an exclusive first interview with someone in the news—think Gary Condit, with whom Connie Chung scored big) and bandwagon coverage of everything from kidnapping sprees to shark attacks, which takes the media's attention away from books—unless you happen to have written a book on people who steal kids or on nasty sea creatures.

Then there's world events, which can, in short, make or break a book. After 9/11, many fiction and general nonfiction (meaning biography, history, literary essays, etc.) authors found it impossible to get any coverage other than reviews. For authors of specialized nonfiction books that don't generally get coverage in book review sections, it spelled disaster. Health columnists were writing about anthrax. Parenting columnists were writing about nightmares and helping children cope with loss. Business columnists were writing about the attack's effect on the market. They weren't covering things like breast cancer, over-homeworked kids, or 401(k)s. They weren't looking to the pile of books they'd just received from publicists for their story ideas. In fact, many of these columnists were pulled off their regular beats to cover the aftermath. Similarly, radio and TV producers weren't looking to their book stacks for show ideas. They had their topics locked in; they just needed the experts. And unless you had written a book on terrorism, grief, or the Middle East, you weren't likely to be tapped. If you *had* written a book on one of those topics, it was now more relevant that ever, and you were in higher demand than you otherwise would have been. But those authors were few and far between. It was a time when publicists went home early . . . and deflated.

During the war against Iraq, some books tanked like so many Bradleys. Serious works of nonfiction that did not relate to the war struggled to get even cursory coverage. The country's thoughts were on the conflict, as were the media's. Books on combat and diplomacy got good play. Authors of foreign policy books received some attention. So too did titles that took on the government or the media's coverage of it—books like Gore Vidal's *Dreaming War*, *Nation* columnist Eric Alterman's *What Liberal Media?*, and Michael Moore's *Stupid White Men*, all three of which made the *New York Times* bestseller list (Moore's book climbing to the number one spot, despite—or perhaps because of—his Oscar acceptance speech). Eventually, as the war dragged on, readers and the media started to look for an escape, and interest in novels began to pick up. But by then, many tours had already been cancelled, and many copies had been packed and returned.

Two instances in which books were not packed up and returned occurred back-to-back in June of 2003 with the release of Hillary Clinton's memoir, *Living History*, and the fifth book in the Harry Potter series, *Harry Potter and the Order of the Phoenix*. For a couple of weeks, the media focused almost all of their book coverage on these titles. Just as an example, *On Point*, which airs on Boston NPR affiliate WBUR, spent almost half of their hour-long summer reading roundup discussing these two tomes (*USA Today* Book Critic Deirdre Donahue, *Time* magazine Book Critic Lev Grossman, and Harvard Bookstore VP of Merchandising Carole Horne were the guests). While the release of these books was much celebrated by sales execs in publishing houses across America (after all, they increased bookstore traffic quite a bit), for publicists of other books it was tough-going. Any time a book becomes "the book," it dwarfs all other titles.

THE STATE OF THE BOOK REVIEW

Reviews are a key component of publicity for certain kinds of books. In recent years, many magazines and newspapers have pared down or even gotten rid of their book review sections. For example, the *Boston Globe*, which used to have a stand-alone books section, now has only a few pages in the back of their Sunday "Ideas" section. They still run daily reviews, but no longer on Fridays or Saturdays. The *Wall Street Journal*, known for its one-a-day reviews, no longer offers this daily vitamin on Mondays. The *Philadelphia Inquirer* has dramatically reduced its Sunday "Books" section, as has the *San Francisco Chronicle* (which folded its stand-alone book review section into another Sunday section until public outcry forced a return to the original format; at present it's still separate, but noticeably thinner).

This downsizing of book coverage is the product of a lackluster economy. Advertising dollars are hard to come by, so pages have to be cut. In an effort to cram more into less, reviews are the first to go. What does this mean to you? Competition is keener. In lieu of a review you'll need off-the-book-page press. You may have to rely on blurbs instead of quotes for ad copy. And a bad review hurts more since fewer good ones will offset it.

Some book review editors seem committed to covering the same number of books, despite their reduced number of pages. That means reviews are shorter. Consequently, they're often merely descriptive, which makes them much less "selling." You're more likely to see a line like "This is the tale of a man who goes hunting" than "This is a book you must go out and buy." And it's the latter that makes readers take notice.

WHAT BOOK P.R. IS *NOT*

Along with understanding what book publicity is, it's important to understand what book publicity—a.k.a. book P.R.—is not. It's not something that's designed to grow your consulting business or sell your corporation's product. It's not geared toward making you famous or raising your speaker's fee. While it may have those effects, the ultimate goal of book publicity must be to sell your book.

Publishing is, after all, a business. The days of publishing a book because it deserves to be published are (I hate to say it) over. Houghton Mifflin, the publisher of Henry David Thoreau, was until just recently owned by Vivendi, a French multi-media conglomerate; Little, Brown is parented by Time-Warner, which recently tried to sell off its entire book publishing division. More than ever before and more than they should be, books are seen merely as a vehicle for profit. Numbers are crunched when a book is signed, when a book is promoted, when the paperback's sold. If your book doesn't sell, it may be remaindered (sold at or near unit cost so the publisher breaks even). The editing may be "streamlined," so to speak, if more revision time would jeopardize the scheduled pub date (some distributors fine publishers when a title comes off press late).

With all of this in mind you, the author, must make *selling* your book your number one priority. That's what will please your publisher; that's what will make them want to publish you again. And, if you decide to go elsewhere with your next book, you'll need to have a good sales track in order to interest another house.

So get out there. Sell your book. If it's good, you won't feel like you're selling your soul in the process.

Chapter 2

The Publicity Process

Though the publicity process for every book will always differ slightly, certain things tend to happen at rather predictable times. Here's an overview of what you can expect—and also what you should be looking for, insisting on, and doing—during the life of the promotion of your book.

MAKING CONTACT

Authors are often puzzled as to why they don't hear from their publicist the minute their contract is signed. The truth is, publicists tend to be rather strategic about when they first make contact. Opening the lines of communication opens up the floodgates for questions and ideas for which the publicist may not be ready. The publicist needs time to become familiar with the project—to read the proposal if she hasn't already done so; to read at least some of the book. The publicist also needs time to gather her thoughts about what opportunities exist before she can entertain the thoughts of the author. Furthermore, the publicist is probably working on other books that just pubbed. Her attention needs to remain on them. Be patient; your time will come.

Keep in mind, too, that editors sometimes ask publicists to delay reaching out to an author so that the author can concentrate on finishing the manuscript. Publicists are usually happy to oblige because it's in their own best interest. After all, if the manuscript is delayed, it means the book is delayed. And if the book is delayed, it messes up the publicist's plans.

So when should you expect to hear from your publicist? Most publicists make contact four to six months before a book pubs—in advance of when bound galleys go out to the media. Bound galleys are down-and-dirty versions of your book that look like cheap paperbacks. There's often no art on the cover, just text. They're for the media's eyes only; they help the media plan ahead.

If you haven't heard from your publicist and are getting concerned, just let your editor know. She, or he, can make the introduction. At the least, your editor will give you your publicist's name, number, and e-mail address. I always think e-mail is the best way to reach out initially. It gives your publicist one last chance to collect her thoughts (and to read a bit of your manuscript if she hasn't already done so) before speaking with you. In the e-mail, just ask if there's a good time you could call to discuss the plans for your book. Don't launch into your ideas yet or she'll think you'll be a handful.

THE AUTHOR QUESTIONNAIRE

An author questionnaire is a form you fill out, often several pages, that provides your publisher with basic background information (your date of birth, alma mater, occupation, etc.) as well as your ideas about promotional opportunities for your book—everything from who might be willing to blurb it, to stores or catalogues that should definitely carry it, to organizations that might want to purchase large quantities of it.

Many houses ask authors to fill these questionnaires out several months prior to publication. The publicist will be particularly interested in the list of your media contacts. Try to provide as much information as possible for each: name, affiliation, physical address, e-mail address, and phone and fax numbers. It's not fair to just give names and expect your publicist to do the research for you. If certain publications or shows have actually covered your work in the past, note that and provide the date.

MEETING WITH YOUR PUBLISHER

It's always a good idea for authors to meet with their publicist and the rest of the publishing team. This is an instance where I recommend you push to get a date set. The meeting doesn't have to be a formal strategy session in the conference room. Sometimes, lunch at a nice restaurant works just as well—or even better. The main thing is for you to get to know them and for them to get to know you. It lays a good foundation on which to build a strong working relationship, and it allows you to get an idea of the amount of time, effort, and money they'll spend on your book so that you can make supplemental plans, if necessary.

Your editor can help you set this up. If your editor seems hesitant, ask your agent to get involved. But do not ask your agent to attend. You need to establish these relationships yourself. You can discuss what the publisher promised with your agent at a later date.

THE CATALOGUE MAILING

Most publicity departments mail their seasonal catalogues to the media with a checklist request form on which the media can indicate which books they'd like to see. The response they get gives them a good idea of the initial interest in your book. So ask your publicist which publications and shows have requested a copy. It'll help you see where it's striking a chord, and you can use it to make sure those contacts receive follow-up at a later date.

MEDIA VISITS

Many publicists call on the media—primarily book review editors and radio and TV producers—on a regular basis, much like a traveling salesman peddling his wares. It's rare that these meetings are for just one title, though for a lead title it's not unheard of. But most of the time these appointments are to present a whole list. Because of time constraints, not all titles are pitched. Those that are often receive under a minute apiece. Generally, the media smiles and nods, and doesn't make a commitment. However, publicists are often able to gauge what resonates and what does not, and scribble notes in their catalogue so that they remember later.

Sometimes, these sit-down meetings with the media occur at the annual national booksellers convention—Book Expo America—or at annual regional book conventions such as those for NEBA (New England Bookseller's Association) or NCIBA (Northern California Independent Booksellers Association). But more often these meetings occur at the book review editor or producer's office. Feel free to ask your publicist whether she makes these kinds of visits, and what kind of feedback she received if she's made them recently.

THE MANUSCRIPT MAILING

Certain monthly magazines have what is commonly referred to as a "long lead time"—often four to six months. For these publications, it's Christmas in July—meaning they start working on their December issue in the middle of the summer. Because of their lead times, these magazines—which include everything from Cosmo and Elle to Esquire and GQ—can't always wait for a bound galley. Consequently, publicists often send them loose leaf manuscripts to look at. This rattles authors because the material is sometimes still a work in progress. But it's necessary and isn't something you should fight. Rest assured these publications understand that the book isn't done yet.

After mailing your manuscript to these magazines, your publicist will follow up to ascertain the recipient's level of interest and try to talk them into coverage.

BOOKING THE TOUR

If you're being sent on a tour for your book, or even if you just want to give talks in your hometown, timing is everything when it comes to securing events. Bookstore calendars fill up fast, particularly in the Fall (publishing's peak season). It's not uncommon for stores to have a three- to four-month lead time. Lecture series at major libraries and museums—and venues like San Francisco's Commonwealth Club, Chicago's Union League Club, and New York's 92nd Street Y—tend to fill up even further in advance. For this reason, your publicist may start to seek commitments even before the galley stage. You can help by letting your publicist know your schedule for the months following your book's release. Hopefully, it will be pretty clear so that your publicist has options. Realize that to keep costs down, your publicist will try to piggyback cities, arranging the schedule so that you go from town to town, rather than home in between. That means she'll need some solid blocks of time to play with.

THE GALLEY MAILING

When galleys are imminent—usually three or four months before your book pubs—your publicist will start to craft the document (known simply as the "galley letter") that will accompany them when they go out to the media. Using her own media database but also the web and reference books like *Bacon's Media Directory*—as well as your suggestions—she'll pull her galley mailing list (affectionately referred to in the biz as just the "galley list").

Anticipate that your publicist will only have a limited number of galleys to work with—as few as a hundred; usually no more than three hundred—and that galleys, as weird as it sounds because they're so darn ugly, actually have a higher unit cost than finished books. This is because they're printed in much smaller quantities; there's no volume discount, so to speak. This means that every golden galley matters. Expect your publicist to send you *one*. Your friends and family will have to wait, as will your colleagues, your boss, and your significant other. Tell your priest or rabbi to get in line.

Your publicist will probably set aside a half dozen—maybe a dozen—galleys to use for her follow-up. It's not unusual for book review editors to claim they never received the first galley sent to them. They're not disorganized; they're simply buried in books.

Sometimes, in lieu of galleys, publishers opt for ARCs (advance reading copies—they look so nice they're sometimes mistaken for paperbacks). Your book's marketing manager will send them to key booksellers to get them excited about the book, and will print enough copies so that they can be given out at various bookseller conventions. If your book has a beautiful cover, and if it's an excellent reading book (like a memoir or a novel), it's a good candidate for an ARC—especially if it's a lead title. If ARCs are being done, your publisher will print enough so that your publicist can use the ARCs instead of galleys for her mailing.

Most galleys (and ARCs) will have the phrase "Uncorrected Page Proofs" emblazoned across them. This is publicist-speak for "Don't you dare quote from this." It signals the media that certain passages may be cut, added to, or otherwise modified, and that there's still proofreading to be done (so don't worry about typos). It means that they are obligated to check against the finished book before writing about it or reading from it on air. The media knows this, and very rarely breaks the code. By and large, they happily conspire to keep your unfinished art safely hidden from public view.

In addition to the galley letter, your publicist may opt to include other material with your galley—like a Q&A (also known as a "self interview"), a full-page bio, or some talking points. She may just staple it all together, or she may put it in a folder (in which case it's called a "press kit"). Some publicists prefer to save this material for the finished book mailing. Personally, I like to include it with the galleys. Why not make a great first impression, especially since many places will have yay'd or nay'd coverage by the time of the finished book mailing.

A week or two after the galley mailing your publicist will start to follow up with the media by e-mail and by phone. The follow-up will continue until she has finished books—at which time there will be another mailing, followed by more follow-up.

THE FINISHED BOOK MAILING

The finished book mailing takes place shortly after your book comes off press—about a month before books hit store shelves. It's larger than the galley mailing because it includes media that does not have a lead time. A finished book mailing typically uses around two percent of the initial print run (the number of copies of your book the publisher produces). For a midlist book at a midsized press, this means between 250 and 400 copies. If there's a tour, I factor in an additional twenty-five books per city to hit up local media. Use these numbers as a general guideline, but keep in mind each book is different.

Make sure that when pulling the finished book list your publicist is thinking on the micro level, not just on the macro. This is the time to hit those publications that weren't big enough to warrant a galley—specialty publications that, while they may not have a very high circulation, reach a targeted audience for your book. Think of it like this: if a general-interest magazine has a circulation of one hundred thousand and two percent of them like psychology books, coverage there could lead to the sale of at most two thousand books. If a psychology newsletter reviews your book, and if its circulation is only two thousand, you have the chance of selling (say it with me) two thousand books.

A week or so after the mailing, books start to land at their media destination. This is when, God willing, your publicist's phone starts ringing. This is when the media calls for interviews; for cover art and author photos to run alongside reviews. This is when they email for a second copy to use for a fact-check. At this point silence is deadly. It indicates that the book hasn't struck a chord. It means she'll have to do that much more follow-up. It means she'd better get back on the horn.

THE RELEASE DATE

The release date—also known as the "ship date"—is the day your book leaves your publisher's (or their distributor's) warehouse. From this day, it can take up to three weeks for the books to actually get to bookstores. It's quicker for the independent stores because the chains (Borders, Barnes & Noble, Walden, Amazon, etc.) all have warehouses—and subwarehouses—of their own through which your book must make its way before actually reaching its intended destination. Then it has to be unpacked and placed upon the shelf.

The release date is a date about which the media won't care. It's just good for you to know what it is, and what it means.

THE ON-SALE DATE

This is the date your book is available for sale in bookstores and online. With the exception of a first-serial excerpt and advance reviews in *Publishers Weekly*, *Library Journal*, *Booklist*, and *Kirkus Reviews*, no media for your book should run prior to this date. The reason? When consumers read about your book, or hear about it on the radio, or see it on TV, it stays in their mind for a little while. If, during this time, they can't find your book in stores, they're likely to forget it. Even if they keep looking, they're going to get frustrated. This in turn will frustrate the bookstores, as they try to explain again and again to dismayed customers why your book is not in stock. This can damage your publisher's relationship with the store (or with the whole account if it's a chain).

That said, sometimes the media will say "it's now or never" for coverage, even before books are in stores. And sometimes, it's such a major opportunity you just can't pass it up. That happened to us recently with a book called *Staying Connected to Your Teenager* by Dr. Mike Riera. About two weeks before it shipped, we got a call from *Oprah*. They were doing a show on teens and wanted our author to be the sole expert, on for the full hour. They even promised a shot of the book. The catch—it was taping the following week, to air the week after that. We knew books wouldn't be on shelves, and asked them to delay it. They said that they just couldn't. And so we had a choice. In the end, we went with it—a bird in the hand, as they say. And though we no doubt missed out on some sales, Amazon captured a lot of preorders.

THE PUB DATE

The pub date is the date your book makes its entry into the world. Think of it as its bar mitzvah, or debutante ball. The date isn't particularly important to the consumer or even to the bookstore, but the media makes careful note of it and bases many decisions on it—decisions like which issue your book gets reviewed in, and when your interview airs.

Pub dates are rather arbitrary. I tend to make them the first or fifteenth of the month just for memory's sake, unless there's a compelling reason not to (for example, a biography of Abe Lincoln that comes out around his birthday; a book about the Irish that hits stores around St. Patrick's, a book about D-Day that's on shelves for June 6th).

The pub date will always fall on or slightly after the on-sale date. For an author, it's a great excuse to go out to dinner. At the very least, buy yourself some roses and pop a little champagne. But don't party too hard; the toughest part's ahead.

THE TOUR / THE INTERVIEWS

Unless your book is fortunate enough to win a major award at a later date—like a National Book Critics Circle or a National Book Award—the month or two after pub date will be your most intense period of interviews. Some of them you'll be able to do by phone (possibly at ungodly hours with interviewers who've clearly not read your book). Sometimes a reporter, or camera crew, or photographer will come out to your house; sometimes you'll have to go to a local studio. And, if you're toured, expect lots of meetings in hotel lobbies, coffee shops, and bars.

It's annoying, it's exhausting. Just try to keep in mind the countless other people who would kill to have this chance, and the tons of potential readers you're reaching.

TAPERING OFF

Eventually—usually two to three months after pub—every book enters what I generally refer to as its "maintenance mode." It's when your publicist handles inquiries from the media but does not actively pursue coverage for you or your book.

You'll probably never actually be told that your book has entered this mode (it feels so rude to tell an author you've stopped working on their book). But you'll notice that your calls won't be returned as quickly if at all. The same holds true for e-mail. You'll start to feel alone. Keep in mind that this is normal although it feels like hell, and that hopefully the success your book has had thus far will keep it going. After all, the best books take on lives of their own. And hey, there's always the paperback!

THE PAPERBACK

Paperbacks usually come off press a year after the book is published in hardcover. If your paperback is published by the same company that published your hardcover, in most instances you shouldn't expect the same level of publicity effort this time around. It's simply not as lucrative for your publisher. If paperback publicity generates a thousand-copy sale, your publisher stands to make $10,000 to $15,000, depending on the list (the suggested retail) price. The same campaign for a hardcover can generate the same thousand-copy sale, but it would make your publisher $20,000 to $30,000 in some cases because the list price of a hardcover is sometimes double that of the paperback. What's more, publicity for a paperback is harder to get for the simple reason that the book is not new news.

Authors often ask me whether they'll be assigned a new publicist for the paperback or continue working with the same person who handled the press for their hardcover. It varies from house to house. When I worked at Houghton, the paperbacks were always handled by the assistants. At Perseus, I handled the paperback of every hardcover I promoted. I encourage you to push for what you think is best. A new publicist could be a good idea because she'd bring a fresh approach even though she may not be a very seasoned staffer. On the other hand, it might be nice to have a publicist who knows your book and its history—a publicist with whom you've already established a relationship and worked out any communication kinks. Just keep in mind that your paperback is unlikely to be your publicist's top priority if she's the person who handled your hardcover because clearly she's used to working on hardcovers and paperback originals, for which expectations are higher and efforts are skewed accordingly.

Of course, if rights to your paperback have been sold to another house, you'll have a new publicist to work with and the level of effort she puts forth might be somewhat greater. Encourage her to speak with your hardcover publicist at some point, just to get a feel for what worked well and what didn't. If you liked the press material for your hardcover, encourage your new publicist to ask your old one for it. No sense reinventing the wheel.

So that's it, in a nutshell. The publicity process. Hopefully, yours will go smoothly from the get go, and your in-house publicist will shepherd you throughout. But in case there are bumps in the road—in case you and your book aren't getting the attention they deserve—the next chapter explores how to get outside help.

Chapter 3

Getting Outside Help

Though dozens of people inside a publishing house work on every book at every stage of the publishing process, it can be necessary—or advisable—for an author to get some outside help when it comes to book promotion. Hiring this help is rarely cheap. In fact, an author could easily spend their entire advance on a freelance publicist alone. For this reason, it's important to identify what kind of outside support will best generate sales for your book or further your career in some capacity—and not empty your pockets.

FREELANCE PUBLICISTS

Sometimes, publishing houses hire freelance publicists for lead books or books that, for one reason or another, will require more time or attention than they anticipate being able to give. Other times, authors hire a freelance publicist when they feel their in-house publicist lacks the skills, time, or dedication it will take to make their book succeed. Either way, it's a major decision—and a major investment.

What They Do

Freelance publicists do much of what in-house publicists do. They research appropriate media for a book, pull together media lists for galley and/or finished book mailings, write press releases and other press material, put together press kits, and pitch and follow up with the media. Some of them will secure media on a city-by-city basis for an author tour (and can even be hired specifically for this purpose), while others prefer to focus on national media. Some freelance publicists will take on an entire campaign—nationals, tour cities . . . the whole ball of wax. When hiring a freelance publicist, it's important to clarify specifically *what* you're hiring her to do. The last thing you want is a misunderstanding that causes a portion of your publicity campaign to go without support, or for her to charge you for the whole kit and caboodle when all you want is help in one area such as radio or TV.

Before hiring a freelance publicist, have a candid conversation with your in-house publicist about what *she* plans to do. In addition to making sure that between the two publicists no publicity stone will be left unturned, it's the only way you can make sure there won't be any duplication of efforts. When it comes to publicists, more isn't better—at least, not if they're targeting the same media. The media resents it when a publicist pitches them a book they've already "passed" on with another publicist, and it does reflect poorly on the author. You don't want the label "media whore."

Keep in mind that, when hiring a freelance publicist, it's important to involve your in-house publicist in the decision-making process. The key is to *ask*, not tell—even if your mind is already made up. Ask if she thinks you should hire one. Ask whom she recommends. Remember, your publisher has made an investment in your book and may be wary about putting all of its eggs in someone else's basket, especially if it's a freelance publicist with whom the in-house publicists haven't worked in the past.

Why and When to Hire One

Not every book can benefit from a freelance publicist. When trying to decide whether or not to hire one, it's important to determine whether your book has true *media* potential. As I mentioned earlier, some books are more dependent on things like grassroots marketing, online marketing, or academic marketing (to generate course adoption). If that's the case with your book, the money you're thinking of spending on a freelance publicist might be better spent elsewhere. Any publicist worth her salt will be honest with you about the media opportunities—or lack thereof—for your particular book. I encourage you to ask a prospective freelance publicist to name a book similar to yours that she has handled, and provide you with a list of the coverage it received.

What are some signs that you may need to hire a freelance publicist? If your publisher has two-page spreads in its catalogue—and if your book isn't one of them—it's probably not a "lead title." That means you may not get the best publicist, or whomever you get may not give it that much attention. If the print run of your book is low compared to other books published there (meaning for a mid- to large-sized press it's fewer than 10,000 copies), again, you may not be your in-house publicist's top priority. If your in-house publicist doesn't return your calls or seems extremely slow in doing so, well, you know what that means—it's time to get more help.

As with most things in life, there are pros and cons to hiring a freelance publicist. On the pro side, it puts you in the driver's seat. Your thoughts and ideas may be more welcome and responded to more quickly. You'll probably receive more updates on progress that has been made, and you'll definitely receive more feedback on passes the media takes. You may have more say in things like press material and "the pitch," as well as more input on what media is approached. Will you get more publicity than you would without this person? Maybe. At least you'll know you tried.

The cons? You could alienate your publicist and the higher-ups on the publisher's staff. Some publishers appreciate it when an author sinks their personal resources into the promotion of their book. Others take it as a lack of confidence in their team. Regardless of how your publisher and publicist view your assistance, never throw it in their face at a later date. A phrase like "I can't believe you're not advertising my book after I spent my own money on freelance help" is not something you want to say. Shelling out your own money on promotion doesn't obligate your publisher to shell out also. Expect the company to stick to its initial budget, which may or may not include an ad.

Another con? Continuity. Or rather, lack thereof. If the publicity for your hardcover isn't handled in-house, come paperback time there won't be a record of who was interested and who was not, which pitches worked and which fell flat. Your paperback publicist will, essentially, be starting from scratch—unless, of course, you re-hire the freelancer who did the cloth campaign. Yes, if you're lucky, the freelancer may be willing to forward a recap. But it can't compare to the "institutional knowledge" that could have been amassed.

Most people enlist the aid of a freelance publicist because they want more attention than their in-house publicist seems able or prepared to provide. It's true that a freelance publicist rarely has as many books on her plate as an in-house publicist. However, realize that you won't be your freelance publicist's only client—and that you may not be her most important one. Keep this in mind when selecting someone. Sure, it'd be fun to be able to say you have the same freelance publicist as John Grisham. But you can bet the majority of the freelancer's time and effort will go his way, and that if it's a big firm they'll put their best person on Grisham's campaign, not yours.

Many authors think that a freelance publicist will be able to spend more time on their book than an in-house publicist because she's not bogged down with things that take time away from pitching—things like meetings to launch a list, and sales conferences. This is true, though a freelance publicist also has to solicit clients—a task that can be quite time-consuming, especially in a down economy.

It's definitely important to carefully time the hiring of a freelance publicist. Generally, the earlier you bring a freelance publicist on board, the more she'll be able to do for you. If you're certain that you want to hire a freelance publicist, I suggest you have her start at the galley stage. However, if you're not sure you need a freelance publicist, you may want to let your in-house publicist take a crack at the publicity first. You can always hire a freelance publicist three months after pub when your in-house publicist starts to turn her attention elsewhere.

However, keep in mind that there's a point after which a freelance publicist can't be of much help. The media likes books that are new (by new I mean no more than six months old). They'll consider covering an older book if it wins an award or suddenly becomes more relevant in light of current events, but otherwise, a book's window of opportunity is fairly small when it comes to the media.

How to Find and Select One

There are several ways to find a freelance publicist. You can look in guides like the LMP (*Literary Market Place*; it's incredibly expensive, but major libraries have it); ask your publisher for recommendations; ask your fellow authors whom they've used; or do research on the Web.

When evaluating whether a particular freelance publicist is right for you, there are several questions to ask. Has she done your kind of book before? Have you heard of the authors with whom she has worked? Has she created bestsellers? Should you go with a big firm like Goldberg-McDuffie or Hilsinger-Mendelson, or would you be better off with a one-person company?

When searching for a freelance publicist, be sure to look for book publicists, not general P.R. firms. Just because they've handled publicity for a company, a product, or a celebrity doesn't mean they know how to publicize a book. Would you hire a podiatrist to remove your appendix just because she has the word "Doctor" in front of her name?

The best way to determine whether a particular publicist is right for you is to ask her to write a proposal. It should outline the media that she'd approach—publications and shows (don't expect to receive the names of her contacts). It should also give you a time-line—when she'd begin and when she'd wrap up. Most books are considered a three-month project; some publicists say four or even six. It should also spell out the intended approach. Would she, for example, be putting you out there as an expert in your field, or would she just focus on getting reviews? Would she try to tie coverage to current events or pitch the story behind the story?

I'm often asked to recommend a freelance publicist. There are many qualified ones out there, but here are a few I've worked with or heard good things about. Please note that the contact information provided below—as well as elsewhere in this book—while accurate at the time of this writing, is subject to change at any moment.

Crane Creek Communications
(specialties: fiction, nonfiction, business, and parenting)
Stephen Crane, P.O. Box 3347, Allentown, PA 18106
Phone: (610) 740-9524
E-mail: stephen@cranecreek.com
http://www.cranecreek.com

Lisa Ekus Public Relations
(specialties: cookbooks)
57 North Street, Hatfield, MA 01038
Phone: (413) 247-9325
E-mail: lisaekus@lisaekus.com
http://www.lisaekus.com

Carol Fass Publicity & Public Relations
(specialties: Jewish-interest books)
26 West 17th Street Suite, 802, New York, NY 10011
Phone: (212) 691-9707
E-mail: info@fasspr.com
http://www.fasspr.com

Susannah Greenberg Public Relations
(specialties: nonfiction, especially business,
health, and Jewish-studies books)
Susannah Greenberg, 26 West 17th Street,
Suite 504, New York, NY 10011
Phone: (212) 208-4629
Email: publicity@bookbuzz.com
http://www.bookbuzz.com

Goldberg McDuffie Communications
(specialties: fiction and serious nonfiction;
has a special division dedicated to business books,
run by Barbara Cave Henricks)
Lynn Goldberg and Camille McDuffie,
444 Madison Avenue, Suite 3300, New York, NY 10022
Phone: (212) 446-5100
Email: bookpr@goldbergmcduffie.com
http://www.goldbergmcduffie.com/

The Hendra Agency
(specialties: business books)
Barbara Hendra, 142 Sterling Place, Brooklyn, NY 11217
Phone: (718) 622-3232
E-mail: bhendra@dti.net

Hilsinger-Mendelson
(specialties: has L.A. and NYC offices
for good coverage on both coasts)
Judy Hilsinger, 6100 Wilshire Blvd.,
Suite 1660, Los Angeles, CA 90048
Phone: (323) 931-5335
E-mail: hmi@hmiwest.com
Sandi Mendelson, 245 Fifth Avenue,
Suite 1401, New York, NY 10016
Phone: (212) 725-7707
E-mail: hmi@hmieast.com
http://www.hilsingermendelson.com

Kim-from-L.A. Literary Publicists
(specialties: fitness and self-help books;
also does media coaching)
Kim Dower, 704 N. Gardner, Suite 4,
Los Angeles, CA 90046
Phone: (323) 655-6023
E-mail: kimfromla@earthlink.net
http://www.kimfromla.com

Krupp Kommunications
(specialties: self-help books—
diet, exercise, relationships, etc.)
Heidi Krupp, 10 West 74th Street,
Suite 1A, New York, NY 10023
Phone: (212) 579-2010
E-mail: HKrupp@KruppKommunications.com
http://www.kruppkommunications.com

Gail Leondar Public Relations
(specialties: political, religious, feminist,
and gay/lesbian books)
21 Belknap Street, Arlington, MA 02474
Phone: (781) 648-1658
E-mail: glpr@aol.com

Sally Anne McCartin & Associates
P.O. Box 1992, Lakeville, CT 06039
Phone: (860) 435-6464
E-mail: samccartin@aol.com

Meryl L. Moss Media Relations
(specialties: nonfiction, especially business books
and business self-help; also provides lecture agent services)
155 Post Road East, Suite 8, Westport, CT 06880
Phone: (203) 226-0199
E-mail: meryl@mediamuscle.com
http://www.mediamuscle.com

Nissen Public Relations
(specialties: nonfiction, especially business books)
Rob Nissen, 2 Central Avenue, Suite 3C,
Madison, NJ 07940
Phone: (973) 410-1234
E-mail: info@nissenpr.com
http://www.nissenpr.com

One Potata Productions
(specialties: style guides)
Diane Mancher, 80 East 11th Street,
Suite 301, New York, NY 10003

Phone: (212) 353-3478
E-mail: OnePotata@aol.com

Jennifer Prost Public Relations
51 Christopher Street, Montclair NJ 07042
Phone: (973) 746-8723
E-mail: jprostpr@comcast.net

Raab Associates
(specialties: children's and parenting books)
Susan Salzman Raab, 345 Millwood Road,
Chappaqua, NY 10514
Phone: (914) 241-2117
E-mail: info@raabassociates.com
http://www.raabassociates.com/books.htm

Rentsch Associates
(specialties: serious nonfiction)
Gail Rentsch, 1841 Broadway, New York, NY 10023
Phone: (212) 397-7341
E-mail: pr@rentschassociates.com
http://www.rentschassociates.com

Toni Werbell Public Relations
(specialties: high-caliber literary fiction and nonfiction)
5 West 86th Street, Suite 4E, New York, NY 10024
Phone: (212) 877-7544
E-mail: twprbooks@aol.com

Jane Wesman Public Relations
(specialties: nonfiction and fiction, especially art and business books; also does radio tours)

322 Eighth Avenue, Suite 1702, New York, NY, 10001
Phone: (212) 620-4080
E-mail: jane@wesmanpr.com.
http://www.wesmanpr.com

Negotiating the Fee and the Focus

So how much does a freelance publicist cost? The answer is, it depends. Most full campaigns (which usually means national print and broadcast as well as media in the top ten to twenty-five markets; it may even include booking media in a few tour cities) generally cost anywhere from $10,000 to $15,000 if it's a small firm and $15,000 to $25,000 if it's a big firm. If the freelance publicist will only be handling the nationals or focusing her efforts on print media (or broadcast media), the fee should be significantly less and will be more open to negotiation. Same goes if she's just booking media for your tour (most freelance publicists charge $1,000 to $2,500 per tour city). As for the pay schedule, most freelancers require half up front and the rest halfway through the campaign. Some will accept the second half upon the campaign's completion. While most freelance publicists with whom I've worked have charged a per-project fee, some prefer to charge on a per-month basis. In that case, I find out how long they think the project will take (three to four months would be the norm) and just do the math to determine final cost.

Before signing a contract with a freelance publicist, make sure it spells out guidelines for expenses so that you don't get stuck with an unexpected bill. It's common for authors to have to pay for shipping costs for galleys and books (be they U.S. mail, UPS, or Fed Ex) and costs associated with press materials (folders, paper, photocopying, author photos, videotapes, etc.). Your publisher might be willing to pick up some of these costs or handle some of the work (for example, in-house staff could do the photocopying or execute the galley or finished book mailings if the freelancer gives them labels), so by all means check. Some smaller P.R. firms may even try to charge you for the calls they make on your behalf, though I feel that should be part of their cost of doing business and recommend you fight it. A "permission" clause is a good idea (meaning they have to seek your permission for expenses over a certain amount—usually $250). A "cap" is also helpful (a line that reads "total project expenses not to exceed X dollars without consultation"; for a full campaign, a normal amount for this would be one to two thousand dollars, though you can certainly try to set it lower if you'd like).

I also recommend that you put an "update" clause in your contract—one that provides for a progress report on a mutually agreed upon schedule. While you won't want your publicist to spend all her time giving you an instant replay of various conversations she's had and e-mails she's received, you also won't want to be left in the dark about the media's response to your book. So I suggest a bi-weekly update. If she balks, monthly updates should suffice.

How can you get your publisher to pay for your freelance publicist? Unless it was the publicity department's idea to hire one, it's never easy. The best way is to get it written into your contract when your book is signed. If it's too late for that, all you can do is try to argue your case, outlining how this person's efforts could generate more sales. If your publisher won't pay for the whole thing, you can try to get the firm to split the cost. At the very least, your publisher should provide the freelancer with the books she requires.

Coordinating Their Efforts with Your Publisher's

Due to cost, you may find it necessary to hire a freelancer using rather narrow parameters (for example, you may contract with them for national media alone). If that's the case, it'll be necessary to divvy up the workload with the in-house publicist. In order to accomplish this, you may want to arrange a conference call with all three interested parties—you, your freelancer, and the person who's in-house.

Even when you hire a freelance publicist to handle the whole project, the in-house publicist may want to retain responsibility for the trades. By trades I mean *Publishers Weekly*, *Library Journal*, *Booklist*, and *Kirkus Reviews*, all of which are published specifically for publishers, booksellers, and librarians—in other words, those in the industry. Because they are so influential—many stores and libraries decide what to purchase based on their reviews—in-house publicists can be loathe to give them up. You should agree to this because the in-house publicist has an ongoing relationship with these publications. There are also some book-specific magazines that you could lump into this category—publications like *Pages*, *ForeWord*, and *BookPage*. And, the in-house publicist may want to retain the right to approach Amazon.com, Borders.com, and BarnesandNoble.com because their coverage may be tied to the number of copies their buyers take (information that's available only to your publisher). Again, you should respect your in-house publicist's wishes.

Consultants and Workshops

If you're not sure you need a freelance publicist but still want a little publicity help, you might want to consider signing up for a book promotion workshop. The cream of the crop? Book Promotion 101 by Bella Stander. Her daylong course is held in a variety of cities (check out her Web site, http://www.bookpromotion101.com, for a list), and covers everything from press material to interview tips. It costs around $200 to $300, and lunch is usually included.

Another option—check with freelance publicists near you to see if they consult.

RADIO AND TV TOURS

If you don't have the money to hire a freelance publicist—or if you feel your in-house publicist has the situation under control—but you still want to give your book an extra push, contracting out for radio or TV satellite tours might be the way to go. They're also good if you want to reach several different geographical markets, but can't or don't want to travel.

So how do these tours work? The company you hire is responsible for securing the interviews and scheduling them. Your in-house publicist provides them with the press material and they go right to work, mailing books, placing calls, and sending e-mails.

For radio tours, you tell them when you want the interviews to happen—specific weeks, or days, or even specific hours. They can cram all the interviews into one or two days if you'd like (which can generate a nice sales "pop"), or spread them out so that they don't significantly disrupt your regular schedule.

Most of the radio interviews will be live, though some of them may be taped. Most will last ten to fifteen minutes but some may go as long as an hour. The majority will be done by phone from your office or your home, though an NPR station may ask you to go to your local affiliate for better sound quality (in which case the company will make the arrangements). In most cases, the station will call you for the interview, though you may, on occasion, be given a toll-free number to dial. The company will see to it that you have the studio numbers handy as a backup. What can you expect during these interviews? There may be listener call-ins or some commercial breaks. It's unlikely the host will have read your book, so don't be surprised or annoyed when his questions are lifted right from your press packet. The good news is, these interviews require no prep at all on your part.

Can any type of book work well for a radio tour? The honest answer is, certain subjects work better than others. Fiction is tough unless you're a famous novelist. Biographies are bad unless the subject is deceased (otherwise, if a show were interested in that person, they'd just ask him or her to be a guest). Books on science, economics, and other high-brow subjects can be a bit of a struggle unless the person booking the tour is targeting NPR. Politics can do okay, especially in an election year. Health, parenting, self-help, technology, and business—particularly personal finance—are all pretty safe bets. I say this because there are lots of shows—subject-specific ones—that focus on these issues, shows with names like "To Your Health," "The Computer Report," or "Family Talk with Dr. Mike." They're hungry for information and knowledgeable author guests. Books on current affairs also work well because general news shows will have you on to discuss what's happening in the world.

A twenty-market radio tour usually costs between $3,000 and $4,000. Tours also come in the forty-market variety. Because they're pretty affordable and the bookings are guaranteed (unlike when you use a freelance publicist who isn't contractually bound to get results), you may be able to convince your publisher to foot the bill. So ask.

A TV satellite tour is considerably more expensive than a radio tour. A ten-market generally runs $7,500 to $10,000 and a twenty-market would run $12,500 to $15,000. Why so high? The studio rental is rather costly.

How do these TV tours work? All of the interviews are done same-day. You go to a local studio and they put you in a room with a cameraman and mike you up. From a control panel on the other side of a glass window, a technician will hook you in to ABC, NBC, CBS, and Fox affiliates across the country—some cable stations, too. There may even be a national channel like CNN. You do the interviews with each network or station back-to-back with sometimes only seconds in between (you may, on occasion, have a five-minute break, but don't count on it—so use the bathroom beforehand!). Most of the interviews will be done live, and since these kinds of segments are usually for mid-morning or noontime broadcasts, these TV tours are almost always conducted between the hours of 10:00 A.M. and 4:00 P.M. Eastern (remember, the stations are throughout the United States).

What type of book works well for a TV tour? A more appropriate question might be would *you* work well for a TV tour? Do you have some TV experience? If you don't, this rapid-fire initiation would be a brutal way to cut your teeth. I would also argue that a TV tour might not be worth the money if you're not already a household name. The more famous you are, the better the markets the company will be able to get. Are "Eyewitness News Topeka" and the like really worth ten thousand dollars?

As with the radio tours, most of the interviewers on your TV tour won't have read your book. I tell all my authors the same thing—if you're asked a stupid question, just answer the question you *should have* been asked.

A final note about radio and TV tours: timing is critical. You want them to coincide with other efforts for your book. So find out when ads for your book will run, when direct-mail campaigns will hit, when your book will be most prominently displayed in chains like Barnes & Noble. And time these tours accordingly. Get the biggest bang for your buck.

Three companies that are well known for these tours (all of them do TV and radio):

Newman Communications
Contact: David Ratner
214 Lincoln Street, Suite 402, Allston, MA 02134
Phone: (617) 254-4500
E-mail: dratner@newmancom.com
http://www.newmancommunications.com

On the Scene Productions
144 East 44 Street, 3rd floor, New York, NY 10017
(They have offices in New York City, Los Angeles,
Seattle, and Chicago)
Phone: (212) 682-5200 (New York office)
http://www.onthescene.com

Planned Television Arts
Contact: Rick Frishman
1110 Second Avenue, 3rd Floor, New York, NY 10022
Phone: (212) 593-5820
E-mail: frishmanr@ruderfinn.com
http://www.plannedtvarts.com

MEDIA COACHES

If you're going to be doing a lot of interviews for your book—
particularly television interviews—and if you're feeling a little anxious about it, you might want to consider hiring a media coach.

A half-day media coaching session—which is usually all it takes to
get you well prepared—generally costs around $3,000. During the
session, the coach asks you questions while the camera rolls, just like a
regular interview. Afterward, together, you view the footage as the coach
points out ways to polish your performance. He'll focus on things like
eye-contact, body language, and speech patterns, but also on the

content, helping you to respond clearly and concisely in a way that's interesting and fresh. He'll also help you figure out how to "bring it back to the book." It's one thing to be a good talking head; it's another to be a good talking head *and* give an interview that generates sales.

Some media coaches will also help prep you to give talks about your book (in bookstores, at conferences and universities, for corporations, etc.). Be sure to ask if that's part of their service before signing. Some of them will also create a demo tape of you being interviewed and/or giving a talk, but it usually costs extra. Though not essential, they're nice to have if your publicist or lecture agent is shopping you around—especially if you don't have other footage.

Will your publisher pay for your media coach? The company may, especially if there's a specific interview for which they want to prep you (something big like the *Late Show with David Letterman*, a morning show, or *Oprah*) or a talk they've booked for you at a major venue (like the National Press Club or the Smithsonian).

Some well-respected media coaches who are used to working with authors:

Biomentary, Inc.
Contact: Bill McGowan
145 Palisade Street, Suite 317, Dobbs Ferry, NY 10522
Phone: (914) 479-0054
E-mail: info@biomentary.com
http://www.biomentary.com

Media Mentor
Contact: Steve Bennett
P.O. Box 382903, Cambridge, MA 02238
Phone: (617) 492-0442
E-mail: steve@mediamentor.com
http://www.mediamentor.com

Parkhurst Communications
Contact: Bill Parkhurst
11 Riverside Drive #1TW, New York, NY 10023
Phone: (212) 362-9722
E-mail: Info@ParkhurstCom.com
http://www.parkhurstcom.com

Perfect Pitch Productions
Contacts: Kim Dower and Bill Applebaum
704 N. Gardner, Suite Four, Los Angeles, CA 90046
Phone: (323) 655-6023 (Kim); (818) 790-3413 (Bill)
E-mail: perfectpitch@earthlink.net
http://www.perfectpitchproductions.com

LECTURE AGENTS

A lecture agent is a person who will approach various universities, corporations, organizations, and conferences on your behalf in an effort to secure paid speaking engagements for you. The reputable ones do not require a fee for this service. Instead, they take a percentage of your speaker's fee: twenty to thirty percent is standard. If this amount sounds high, keep in mind that lecture agents can book you more talks than you can possibly book on your own. They can also get you a higher fee, so in the end you come out ahead.

Unless you're a leader in your field, it will be hard to secure a lecture agent prior to the publication of your book. Lecture agents are choosy. They only take on clients they're certain they can book. However, if you can get one on board early on, they can arrange events to coincide with your pub date. Books can even be sold at these events, and sometimes media can attend them, so it works in your favor on several levels.

To woo lecture agents, you'll need to provide them with footage of you giving a talk to an audience; a tape of TV interviews will not do the trick. They'll need to know the places that you've spoken in the past and the topics you can speak to in the future. If you have a packet of press clips to send them, that can help as well. And if you can't land a lecture agent prior to the pub, feel free to reapproach them once your book is out and getting attention.

In case you're wondering, you should not expect your publicist to secure paid speaking engagements for you. Publicists offer you for free, and usually to different kinds of venues than those the lecture agents book—bookstores and book fairs, primarily.

Lecture agencies that are particularly good with authors include:

The Lecture Bureau
7 Crescent Street, Cambridge, MA 02138
Phone: (617) 492-0355
E-mail: info@thelecturebureau.com
http://www.thelecturebureau.com

The Leigh Bureau
1065 U.S. Highway 22 West, Third Floor, Bridgewater, NJ 08807
Phone: (908) 253-8600
E-mail: info@Leighbureau.com
http://leighbureau.com/lbw

Jodi F. Solomon Speakers Bureau
325 Huntington Avenue, Suite 112, Boston, MA 02115
Phone: (617) 266-3450
E-mail: jodi@jodisolomonspeakers.com
http://www.jodisolomonspeakers.com

Washington Speakers Bureau
1663 Prince Street, Alexandria, VA 22314
Phone: (703) 684-0555
E-mail: info@washingtonspeakers.com
http://washingtonspeakers.com

There's also Charles Lago, whose service is rather unique. In addition to being the events coordinator at Current Affairs Bookstore in San Diego, he has a company called Authors on Tour (http://www.authorsontour.net) through which he books events for authors once the publishers are finished promoting their book. He's particularly good for authors who want to continue touring but whose publishers stop promoting them just as their book seems to be picking up steam. He has a good stable of well-known authors for whom he organizes events around the country—Susan McDougal (*The Woman Who Wouldn't Talk*), Mariel Hemingway (*Finding My Balance*), Heidi Fleiss (*Pandering*), and Arianna Huffington (*Pigs at the Trough*). Part lecture agent, part freelance publicist, he does "pretty much what a publisher's publicist does: I contact bookstores, set up signings, send out press packets, contact media, set up interviews, book travel and hotel, etc." He is able to get some of his authors paid speaking gigs to help offset the costs of their tour.

WEB MARKETERS

Web campaigns are a great way to bring attention to your book, and it's possible to hire someone to do one for you. Check with your publicist first because some of today's publicity and marketing departments have incorporated Web campaigns into their promotional efforts—you don't want to pay for it if it's already being done. However, if it's not, consider enlisting the services of one of these well-connected people. They usually cost around $3,000.

While publicists tend to focus on major sites like Salon and Slate, Web marketers approach a variety of sites on a very grassroots level. For example, if yours is a book about miscarriage, a Web marketer would approach online support groups and fertility-interest sites, as well as general health sites like HealthNewsDigest and WebMD. If yours is a book on praying, they'd go for various church sites and sites like Beliefnet.com. A book on raising teens would mean a push to InfoDad.com, while FrontRangeLiving.com would be approached for books by Colorado authors and tech books would get outreach to FrontWheelDrive.com. Web marketers also target book-specific Web sites like Bookviews.com, Bookslut.com, BookBrowse.com, SirReadaLot.org, and Curl Up With a Good Book (CurledUp.com).

What do these marketers offer to these various sites? Cover art and excerpts, sometimes a canned Q&A. They may suggest you do a chat or moderate a message board. They could talk the site into a review or get you an interview for an article. They could also arrange for the site to link to your book on Amazon.com (or any another online bookstore, including 1800CEOread.com in the case of a business book).

These Web marketers don't usually build you a Web site for your book, but they do make referrals to people who can do that. Here's information on two of the best Web promoters for books, both of whom I've worked with in the past and can vouch for:

FSB Associates
Contact: Fauzia Burke
65 South Maple Avenue, Basking Ridge, NJ 07920
Phone: (908) 204-9340
E-mail: solutions@fsbassociates.com
http://fsbassociates.com

WordTrends
Contact: Peter Costanzo
Phone: (516) 429-1645
E-mail: pcostanzo@wordtrends.com

Whether it's a freelance publicist, radio or TV tour provider, media coach, lecture agent, or Web marketer, outside help can give many books a boost. Dig deep and decide what's right for you based on your expectations, your budget, and what you personally and professionally have riding on this book. Regardless of what you decide, remember to preserve and nurture your relationship with your in-house publicist. More on that in the next two chapters.

Chapter 4

Working with Your Publicist

If you've published with a press that provides a publicist, there are a lot of things you can do to help that person promote your book more successfully.

MAKING YOURSELF AVAILABLE

For the three months before and three months after your book is published, it's best not to take a vacation—unless you plan to promote your book while you're there and have cleared the trip with your publicist before booking it. If possible, lighten your workload so that your schedule will be more flexible for touring (if a tour is planned for your book) and for interviews. If you have a young child and you're the primary caregiver, make sure your partner will have some flexibility in his or her schedule in case interview opportunities present themselves at the last minute. Having a list of babysitters handy is a good idea.

One of my authors had to go on a ten-city tour when her child was two months old. She was breastfeeding, so leaving the child at home was not an option (though we did briefly toy with the idea of Fed-Exing her breast milk back home while she was on the road!). The solution: she hired a nanny to accompany her on some of the tour. For those cities to which the nanny didn't go, I made sure to hire an author escort who liked kids and knew how to change a diaper!

If you do have to be away during this critical window for your book, make sure that you're at least reachable by phone. If you're going to be in a place where you won't have regular access to a phone, try to pre-arrange specific dates and times when you can call your publicist just to check in and see if she needs you.

THE ART OF BEING AGREEABLE

Try to be generous with your time. While it's true that an interview with an AM station in Medina, Ohio at 7:00 A.M. on a Saturday probably won't make your book a bestseller, every little bit of exposure does help. Who knows—maybe the organizer of Medina's best book club will hear you on the show and buy two dozen copies of your novel. Or maybe the CEO of Medina's biggest company will hear you discuss your business book and purchase two hundred copies to give to his clients as Christmas gifts. That's the beauty of doing media—you just never know. So if possible, don't pass up an interview with any reputable media, no matter how small their circulation or viewership or listenership (or how late or early the interview).

Keep in mind, too, that the big shows and publications aren't guaranteed tickets to bestsellerdom. Many authors fall victim to what I like to call the "*Oprah* myth." They think that if they get on *Oprah*—or reviewed in the *New York Times Book Review*—they'll be sitting next to Grisham on the bestseller list. The fact is, not every *Oprah* appearance generates massive sales. In the past four years, five authors whose books we've published have been on *Oprah*—four of them for the full hour, three as the exclusive expert. We certainly saw an increase in sales the week of their appearance (and a smaller but still noticeable jump when the shows re-aired). However, none of the books went on to become bestsellers, despite the ads we ran to coincide with the appearances, the extra number of copies we were able to place in stores, and the other media requests we received in the wake of the broadcasts. And while many of the NYTBR's reviews of our books have generated additional media interest and significant sales bumps, some have garnered nary a call and only a slight blip in sales. So these kinds of hits are not a papal blessing. They don't lead to instant fame, and they won't necessarily change your life. Sure, you want them. I do, too. But you need to be willing to do smaller stuff—not just because the big stuff is hard to get, but because bestsellers are the product of repetition. People need to see your book all over the place before they'll buy it.

It's also important to realize that there's nothing more deflating for a publicist than securing an interview for her author, only to have him or her deem it unworthy. It comes across as ungrateful, no matter how nicely you refuse. So practice the art of being agreeable. Of course, part of this art is keeping requests for reschedulings to an absolute minimum. Some things are unavoidable: authors get sick like everyone else, have family emergencies, get called out of town on business. However, remember that a publicist has only so much time to devote to each book, and each time your publicist has to reschedule an existing interview for you, it's one less new interview she's able to go after. So for your sake as much as hers, avoid asking for a reschedule simply because it would make your life a little more convenient.

MAKING YOURSELF ACCESSIBLE

Try to make it easy for your publicist to contact you if she needs to run an interview date by you in order to book it quickly. Ideally, she'll be able to get in touch with you immediately if, for instance, she has a reporter on deadline who needs to reach you ASAP. You don't want to miss the opportunity for coverage of your book. If you don't have e-mail, this is a good time to get it. If you don't have a cell phone, this is a great time to buy one. Whenever possible, return your publicist's voice-mail messages promptly. And for those of you with kids, make sure they know how to take a good message and that they know to leave it somewhere where you're sure to see it.

If you want instant access to the reviews your book receives, this is a great time to purchase a fax machine. If you don't want to shell out the bucks, get creative. I had one author whose reviews I faxed to his wife's place of business. Another author received some last-minute changes to her tour schedule via her next door neighbor's fax. In a pinch, Kinko's, Staples, and similar stores will accept faxes on behalf of their customers for a nominal fee.

RESEARCHING APPROPRIATE MEDIA

One of the best ways for an author to help his or her publicist is to don a detective's cap. Research appropriate media for your book and give your publicist a list (complete with contact information—she may not be willing or able to take the time to research the address). This list can be part of your Author Questionnaire, or you can send it under separate cover. It should include shows and publications as well as individual producers, reporters, and editors.

For example, an author of mine who wrote a biography of Alan Greenspan gave me a list of reporters who cover the Federal Reserve for the top twenty-five papers in the United States as well as the major wire services. I sent each of them a book, and we got lots of coverage, including an Associated Press article that ran in papers nationwide.

Pulling together a list of the country's major book review editors may not be worth your time, as that's something your publicist will most likely already have. But a list of book review editors at special-interest publications that are right for your book is always helpful. If you wrote a book about coal, you'd want to give your publicist the name of the book review editor at *On Earth*, the magazine of the Natural Resource Defense Council. If you wrote a book on psychology, you'd want to supply info for the books editor at *Psychoanalytic Review*.

If a book similar to yours has come out in the past year or two, it's not a bad idea to do a Web search using Google (http://www.google.com) to see where it was covered and by whom. Make a list for your publicist—again, with contact info.

Also be sure to provide information on your local media—your hometown newspaper, the college radio station on the campus where you teach. And don't forget the alumni mags for the place or places where you got a degree (their circulations are national and big, and most of them have a book review section).

One final note: If you belong to—or know of—any professional journalism societies, let your publicist know. For a reasonable fee, many of these organizations will provide you with a roster of their members (complete with their contact info so that an e-mail blitz or mailing can be done). For example, for two of our recent science books—*Love at Goon Park* by Deborah Blum and *Watson and DNA* by Victor McElheny—we rented the National Association of Science Writers list and used it for postcard mailings (the postcard included my number and e-mail address so that the writers could contact me to request a copy of the book). Back when I was at Houghton Mifflin, we used a similar tactic with a list of education reporters for Alfie Kohn's book *The Schools Our Children Deserve*, using it to mail the book's press release. For business books, you can get a list from the Society of American Business Editors and Writers (http://www.sabew.org).

PROVIDING PERSONAL CONTACTS

If you have any personal media contacts, you should give them to your publicist—preferably as part of your Author Questionnaire, preferably before the galley stage. This includes friends or family who work in the media. Even if they're not in a position to interview you or cover your book, they may be able to hand-deliver it to someone who is. Also provide your publicist with a list of people who have covered you or your work in the past. Your name will be familiar to them, which will make your publicist's job much easier.

WRITING OP-EDS

You can help your publicist by writing an op-ed that somehow connects current events to your book. Your publicist should be able to provide you with a list of op-ed editors at the papers you'd like to approach, as well as their submission guidelines. If not, you can usually get that information off the publication's Web site. Your book's editor should be willing to help you craft the op-ed, and it's not a bad idea for you to run it by your publicist in order to get her take on it. However, when it's ready to go, you should be the one to submit it to the paper. They frown upon submissions from publicists, as it makes it seem like the op-ed is just a vehicle for book (or self) promotion, rather than an impassioned response to current events from an interested reader.

You can also write a newspaper or magazine article that's tied to your book and mentions it in your bio line. Your publicist may have suggestions of publications—and possibly even editors—to approach, though as with op-eds you should do the actual approaching. If necessary, a trip to your local newsstand will provide you with a bunch of good ideas. These op-ed pieces and articles are great to get, as they can be used as a springboard for getting other coverage, particularly on radio and TV.

KEEPING ABREAST OF CURRENT EVENTS

The most media-savvy authors keep their eyes and ears open for things in the news that can serve as hooks for getting publicity for their book. My Alan Greenspan biographer used to give me a heads-up a few days before every big Fed announcement was made, and I was able to use the info to get him on NPR's *Motley Fool* and similar shows to reflect on the Chairman's speech.

On my morning drive down I-93 from New Hampshire into Boston, I listen to NPR to see if anything is going on in the world that one of my authors can speak to. When I get to the office, I spend the first few minutes online, scanning the headlines of *USA Today* and the *New York Times*. But I don't catch everything! There's nothing I like better than an e-mail from an author with a link to an article about a major study that has been released, or some survey results that have just come out. I forward the link to other media with the press material for the book, and frequently I get replies saying "Yes, let's book him."

The more aware you are, the more aware your publicist will be . . . and the more she'll be able to use current events to make the media (and the customer) aware of your book.

HELPING TO CRAFT THE PRESS MATERIAL

Authors can be a real asset to a publicist when it comes to preparing the press material for their book. Ask if she wants your help beforehand to make sure, but your publicist will probably appreciate your providing her with a full-page bio (no one knows your accomplishments as well as you do), some talking points ("Ten Reasons to Talk with Your Teenager About Sex," "Five Alternatives to the 401(k)"), and a self-interview (a.k.a. a Q&A).

Some books will require a full-blown press kit—a folder that contains lots of "stuff" about you and the book. Other books—

such as those titles which are more academic—can get by with a simple press release, or a bunch of stapled pages (their subject matter and scholarship is sufficiently impressive; they don't need the glitz and glam of a press kit). Ask your publicist what she thinks is appropriate for your book. Personally, when it comes to press material, I believe size matters. While I don't advocate sending extraneous material, I do advocate sending a substantial amount of material. My experience has been that the media gives more attention to books that have press kits.

So what constitutes useful and attention-grabbing press material? Let's take it item by item.

Press Release

- A press release gets sent out with every finished book that goes to the media, so it's very important to have an impressive one.
- Rule number one: try to keep it to a page. The media is inundated, and they're quick to lose patience and interest in a press release that's too long. At most, your release should be two pages.
- Avoid praising the book—that's the media's job; make the book sound interesting and important—don't just say it is. Avoid adjectives. Avoid hype.
- Give the release a headline—either the title of the book or a brief explanation of what the book does ("New Book Explores the History of Britain," "First-Time Novelist Sheds Light on Southern Families," "Biography Questions How Star Got Debut Role," "Children's Book Teaches Tolerance").
- For nonfiction, put the book in some sort of current context. Make it timely. For example, "As dignitaries gather in

New York for the World Economic Forum, author X explores the economic ramifications of . . ."

- Include the book's "specs" and don't make the media hunt for them—title, subtitle, author, price, ISBN, number of pages, dimensions (especially important for art books), name of publisher, pub date (for hardcovers and paperback originals, make sure it's at least a month from the date the media will receive it).

- Make sure contact information (which should include your publicist's phone, fax, address, and e-mail) is highly visible.

- If you know your book has competition (in other words, if there's a similar book pubbing around the same time), take a sentence or two to explain how yours is different. This may result in your book being paired in reviews with the other book—but it's better than having them only review the other book or overlooking both of them. Remember, book review editors love to pair books for review; it can really increase your chances of coverage. Also, reporters love to do trend pieces, and two books on a similar topic equals a trend.

- Proofread so that you catch the typos. Don't just spell check. If you can get a friend or colleague to proof it, too, that's great. The more eyes, the better. Of course, your publicist will proof it, as well.

Author Bio

- Tell where you currently live, by whom you're currently employed, and your official title.
- Mention your previous books, any bestseller lists they were on, and any awards your previous books received. If

you've received non-book-related awards, mention them, too, if they're relevant to the subject of your book.

- If your work has been published in national magazines and papers, or on major Web sites (like Salon.com), mention a few of them. But don't bother to list obscure publications or highly academic journals. Great if you've been published in *Glamour* or the *New Republic* or the *Wall Street Journal*. Not so great if you've been published in the *Journal of Ambulatory Pediatrics*.

- If it's a parenting book, mention how many kids or grand-kids you have. If it's a book about animal rights, list your pets. If it's a book about Italy, tell us you were born there or travel there each winter. But in general, avoid extra-neous personal details.

- Remember, the goal of the bio is twofold: to make you sound like the premier expert on the topic, and to make you sound like an interesting person.

Q&A or List of Questions

- Whenever possible, include a Q&A in your press kit. Title it "A Conversation with (insert name), Author of (insert book title)" or something similar. It gives the media a good feel for what you sound like (be sure to use your own voice—try not to sound rehearsed or too formal) and what you have to talk about. To get started, simply list a dozen or so questions (your publicist may even be willing to supply them for you). Then answer each query in five to seven sentences. If you don't have the time to do the answers, at least create a sheet of questions to include. Q&As and questions are especially useful for radio pro-ducers and hosts who rarely have time to actually read the book, and may cause them to choose your book over one for which they'd have to do more prep work. If your book tackles complex material, Q&As or questions are an absolute must if you want to get some bookings.

• Avoid run-of-the-mill questions like "What's Your Book About?" and "Why Did You Write This Book?" Wouldn't you rather read the answer to "Why would someone with schizophrenia in America today be worse off than a person in a third-world country twenty years ago?" or "Is it true you got your idea for this novel while backpacking in the Himalayas?"

Here's what some members of the media have to say about Q&As and lists of questions:

"I sometimes use the questions that publicists provide. However, when I feel that the questions are dopey, fluffy, self-serving, and are designed to sell books rather than educate the audience, I often dump the whole thing."

—Armin Brott, host of *Positive Parenting* (KOIT Radio, San Francisco)

"I always write my own questions, but I do appreciate it when publicists send their questions. It helps to know what other people find important or interesting. I find it also helps me keep my questions from becoming too esoteric."

—Annette Heist, producer at National Public Radio's
Talk of the Nation Science Friday

"I always make up my questions before looking at the ones provided by publicists, because I want the questions to come out of my own curiosity or journalistic motives. Sometimes I never look at the publicist's questions. Sometimes I look to see if there is autobiographical info there so that I don't have to spend the short interview time asking that. I tend to look at the publicist's questions if I didn't connect with a book. When I like or admire the book, my own curiosity is enough. When I'm bored or not moved by a book, I need help finding a way in sometimes."

—Robin Dougherty, "Between the Lines" columnist for the *Boston Globe*'s Sunday "Books" section

"I nearly always make up my own questions, because those provided are rarely really, really good (it does happen that they are, just rarely). I do, however, carefully review press materials so that I don't repeat common questions, get facts wrong, or miss a fact/idea that I can use to build a new question. I have colleagues who never read these materials because they're afraid doing so will stifle their question-crafting abilities."

—Bethanne Kelly Patrick, Editor-at-Large, *Pages* magazine

Though different members of the media use Q&As and lists of questions in different ways and with varying frequency, it's clear that they do appreciate receiving them. So do what you can to oblige.

Sheet of Media Praise for Your Previous Book(s)

- The media may not read what the reviewers had to say, but they'll definitely look at which publications reviewed it, so only include quotes from the best places—national magazines and papers, major-market papers, and major Web sites.
- If the review was written by a well-known critic or reviewer, list his or her name, not just the name of the publication (for example, say Richard Eder, the *New York Times*—not just the *New York Times*).

- If there were large, glowing reviews in major places, include the whole review in the press kit—don't just quote from it.

Sheet of Advance Praise for Your New Book
- Include endorsements (a.k.a. blurbs) from high-profile authors and opinion-makers only. A general rule of thumb: if your next-door neighbor has never heard of them, neither has the media.
- Include quotes from advance reviews in *Publishers Weekly*, *Kirkus Reviews*, *Library Journal*, and *Booklist*. If the entire review is good, put the whole thing in the kit.
- Avoid quoting online booksellers like Amazon.com. They're in the business of selling books, so everyone assumes (true or not) that they're going to write favorable reviews.
- Avoid quoting major publications that have run their reviews early. If you quote *Fortune* or *Forbes*, *Business Week* may feel scooped when they get the press kit, and may be less likely to cover your book.

Talking Points Sheets
- Expect (and encourage) these to be reproduced verbatim by the print media. Unfortunately, you won't get paid when they run it, but it'll be good promo for your book.
- Think of these as lists and title them as such—"Ten Things to Look for in a Daycare Center," "The Common Mistakes Women Make When Investing," "Top Concerns on the Minds of America's CEOs," "The Warning Signs of Alzheimer's Disease," "Five Ways Global Warming Is Harming the Environment."

Excerpt

- For fiction: what better way to show the power of your prose than to point the media directly to a lovely or poignant passage?
- For nonfiction: this is especially useful for elegant prose about a complex subject. It's a quick way of showing that in addition to being a brain, you can actually write. Pick a passage or two that reads well, can stand alone, and is intriguing or controversial. If it represents the book's main idea, all the better.
- The excerpt(s) should take up no more than one sheet in the press kit.

Author Photo

- If yours is not a review-driven book, there's usually no need to include an actual photo in what you send to the media. They'll speak up if they need one, and major magazines and papers almost always take their own shots for off-the-book-page coverage. I do, however, suggest you make your photo a component of the bio page—especially if your photo isn't on your book.
- If your book is review-driven, if at all possible, include an actual photo (especially if you're a first-time author who is striving to break out . . . and especially if you're camera-friendly). If you have a press kit, just tuck it inside the folder. If not, tuck the photo in the front of your book so that it doesn't get bent during shipping.

Folders/Press Kit Covers

- Custom folders that reproduce or incorporate elements of

your book's cover design are great. They're also expensive. If money is an issue, a plain folder will suffice.

- If there's a little extra to spend, have "crack and peel" labels of the cover made and affix them to a plain folder (preferably a glossy one—they "pop" a little more). Another possibility: card-stock covers that can be stapled right to the press material. They can be done—cheaply and quickly—at most copy shops.

Miscellaneous Words of Advice

- Prepare your press kits early. Your publicist should send as much of the material detailed above as possible with the galley or manuscript *and* the finished book. If it's just sent with the finished book, some of the media won't see the most impressive material until it's too late for them to assign the book for coverage.
- If your publicist agrees, run your press material by your book's editor before it goes out to make sure you've honed in on what makes your book unique. You may be too close to the book to know what makes it special.

PROVIDING A VIDEOTAPE AND PHOTO

Your publicist will need you to provide a nice (preferably professionally taken) black-and-white photo of yourself—and possibly also a color one. Send them to her as hard copies but e-mail them to her as jpegs and/or tif files, too. This will make it that much easier for her to provide the print media with the artwork they need to accompany their reviews and profile pieces. Illustrated articles are read more often than ones that aren't illustrated as the art draws people's attention to them. So it's worth the extra effort and expense (the publisher usually won't pay for the sitting). Be sure to provide the photo credit (the name of the person who took the shot).

Your publicist will probably also appreciate a tape of previous TV interviews you've done. She can use it to "sell" you to producers at the morning shows, talk shows like *Oprah* and *The View*, and evening newsmagazines like ABC's 20/20, CBS's *60 Minutes*, and NBC's *Dateline*. If you haven't been on TV before, have a friend or relative videotape you answering some questions about your book, and send that to your publicist. It's definitely better than nothing. And, if you have some extra money to spend, there are companies that specialize in helping authors create promo tapes.

If you have videotape of yourself giving a presentation or speech, offer it to your publicist, even if it doesn't pertain to your book. It may be helpful if she's trying to book major speaking engagements for you, as it would showcase your delivery skills and ability to captivate an audience.

HELPING WITH THE FOLLOW-UP

Your publicist may want you to help follow up with your personal media contacts (and *only* your *personal* media contacts) after galleys and/or finished books are sent. I find e-mail to be a particularly good method for this. Keep it low-key—something along the lines of "Hi Ken. I asked my publicist to send you a copy of my new book, *The Best Book in the World*. So let me know if you didn't get it. Hope you like it.—John." In a perfect world, this will generate a response along the lines of "Hi John. Got the book. It looks awesome! Hey, can I interview you about it?" or "Hi John. The galley has arrived. Passed it to Jed at our sister mag with a rec that he review it." In other words, the media knows what you want without your asking for it.

SHARING CLIPS

Help your publicist by looking for coverage of your book on a daily basis after it has pubbed. Sign up for Yahoo News Alerts, a service that e-mails you when articles containing your specified search term(s) run. It misses things, to be sure, but it's free and easy. Make use of free news search-engines, like Dogpile.com, News.Google.com, and WorldNews.com. There's also one on CNN.com's "Industry Watch" (http://cnniw.yellowbrix.com) that's particularly good for obscure publications. Another option is to subscribe to Lexis/Nexis; it's expensive but more comprehensive. For each of these, be sure to search for both your name and the name of your book. If it's more than one word, put the title in quotes to reduce extraneous material. Whatever you find— especially if it's national—share it with your publicist immediately so that she can use it to get more coverage, and so that she can get word to the sales force who in turn can alert the stores.

Another good trick—take advantage of "advance title lists" that appear on the Web sites of certain publications. On the Web site of *Kirkus Reviews*, for example, you'll find a list of the reviews slated for their upcoming issue (http://www.kirkusreviews.com). It's updated every couple of days as, in the words of Chuck Shelton—who assigns all of their nonfiction titles—"the issue grows and grows." *BookPage* also provides a good one (http://www.bookpage.com/advance/). And every Friday, *Publishers Weekly* provides a list of the titles that will be reviewed in Monday's issue at http://www.publishersweekly.com (just click on "Forecasts"). But the mother of all advance title lists definitely appears courtesy of the American Booksellers Association's *Bookselling This Week* in their "Media Guide" section (http:// news.bookweb.org/mediaguide). You can type the name of your book in their search box, or you can scroll through the print, TV, and radio lists to see what's coming up.

Some newspaper and magazine reporters are good about mailing tearsheets (the actual pages on which the coverage appears) to authors whom they've interviewed. If you get a hard copy of a review or article before your publicist does, fax it to her or pop a copy in the mail. She'll be grateful to have it—especially if her clipping service misses it or is slow.

The Author/Publicist Dynamic

If you took a look at my Christmas card list, you'd see it peppered with poets and essayists, scientists and doctors, and others whose books I've publicized. I don't send them holiday greetings because I feel the need to butter them up. It's not an olive branch, or some sort of networking thing. These are people I care about—people who have made important contributions to literature and also to my life. I'm pleased to say I get cards from a lot of them, too.

Your publicist could take her people skills, her writing skills, her lovely phone manner, and her media contacts, throw in her publishing towel, and do corporate P.R. She'd probably double her salary. But I doubt she'll ever do it. She loves books way too much. To her, a famous CEO can't hold a candle to a debut novelist.

Oh, but you authors aren't easy! You drink too much at your wine and cheese receptions. You burst into tears when you get a bad review. You get high and forget your 7:00 A.M. phoner. ("My God," you say, "why'd you schedule it so *early?*" Because it's drive-time—that's when they do it . . . *live.*)

Still, you're worth it. I'm yours, and you are mine—assuming, of course, we don't *completely* piss each other off.

THE IMPORTANCE OF THE PUBLICIST

Publishing is a business of personal relationships. Editors and authors often form tight bonds. So do publicists and authors. But even more than your editor, your publicist is in a position to be your greatest champion—in-house, with the sales force, and with the media. In short, she can make or break your book. Never lose sight of this fact.

Keep in mind, too, that proposals are often circulated to publicists—or at least to the director of publicity—before books are acquired. They're invited to weigh in on a book's media potential long before it's actually a book. For this reason, if you think you might want to do another book with your current house, you need to keep your publicist in your good graces. If she tells the other decision makers you're media-savvy—or even just a dream to work with—it will carry weight and could help to offset things like your previous book's poor sales track or negative reviews.

NURTURING YOUR RELATIONSHIP WITH THE PUBLICIST

If you can see your publicist is working hard for you, be sure to tell her thanks. Maybe even send her a thank-you note when you return from your tour or when she lands you a solid booking. Better yet, send her flowers or chocolate or a gift certificate for a massage (trust me, she could use one). Showing your appreciation of her abilities and her effort will make her work harder for you, even if your book is not an in-house priority. Also, give credit where credit is due, and do so publicly. When your book hits a bestseller list, send your publicist a thank-you e-mail—and cc your editor and the publisher. If you make her look good, she'll return the favor—guaranteed.

Never hold your publicist accountable for a bad review. Publicists have some sway when it comes to convincing a publication to review your book, but they cannot choose who reviews it or what they have to say about it. Their job is—and can only be—to get your book coverage. Not positive coverage. Coverage.

When it comes to your publicist, check your ego at the door.

You work for her and her employers, not the other way around. I will never forget a certain famous historian who actually demanded I get him coffee (I was just about to offer; I told him we were out). Contrast that with John Kenneth Galbraith who invited me to his garden party—me, at the time a twenty-six-year-old no one, eating cucumber sandwiches with Julia Child and his other Cambridge guests! Want to guess whose book got more of my positive energy—whose book went on to become a bestseller?

No, you don't have to bribe your publicist with invites to lavish lawn parties. But common courtesy and a little respect sure do go a long way. And the occasional box of macaroons—also very helpful.

Keep in mind, too, that the road to a good relationship with your publicist can be paved by others with whom she works. In short: people talk. If you've been nice to the art director when discussing cover concepts; if the production team mentions that you met all their deadlines; if your editor comments that you take criticism well—all of these things will help you get off on a good foot with your publicist. Conversely, if everyone agrees that you've been a bear, forget it. Your publicist will have her guard up long before you meet. She may never get past what she heard about you in the ladies room.

ASSESSING YOUR PUBLISHER'S AND PUBLICIST'S COMMITMENT

The more closely you work with your publicist, the more you'll see that she has many masters. She's responsible for producing results for her immediate supervisor, the marketing team, the publisher, the sales force, and the editors (whose reputations ride on the success of the books they acquire), as well as for you and her other authors. Expect her to parcel her efforts based on which books are in-house priorities. If you want to know whether your book is an in-house priority, check out the catalogue. Does your book have a double-page spread? Is the announced first printing significantly larger than that for other books? Do they have a big ad campaign planned for it? Are they touring you? Are they doing reading samplers for your book? Are they printing advance reading copies (ARCs) instead of regular galleys? Not all of these things are applicable for all books, but in general they're signs that your book is a key one for that season and that your publicist will pull out all the stops to make it work.

THE PUBLICIST'S PERSONALITY

I'll be the first to admit that publicists aren't the easiest bunch to work with. We are by nature a headstrong lot. Try not to forget you want that. It's what keeps us picking up the phone to call the media about your book. We're used to getting rejected all day long, and have developed a pretty thick skin. So if we seem abrupt or a tad inflexible, please don't take offense. It doesn't mean that we're not working hard to promote your book.

Above all else, remember that your publicist is a professional, just as you, the author, are a professional. She would not presume to know how to write your book and, though you will have many helpful ideas, she may bristle if you presume to know how to publicize it. Little tricks like phrasing things in the form of a question can go an awfully long way toward turning know-it-all commands into gently persuasive suggestions: "Do you think we should try for NPR?" "Is this a hook for Nightline?"

It helps endear you to your publicist if you express an understanding of the intricacies of book publicity. For example, timing is everything. The coverage must not run before books hit stores—but must run soon thereafter if it is to have significant effect on sales. Also, there's a hierarchy for certain kinds of coverage: KGO in San Francisco insists on being the first live Bay Area radio interview, and the *Boston Globe* won't run a profile piece if the *Boston Herald* has already done so; *USA Today* won't do an article on the heels of a morning show interview (they'd want to run the day before so they could "break" the story).

It's also important to keep in mind that, no matter how much of a go-getter she is, a publicist only has a certain amount of hours to devote to promoting each book. Don't be offended if she sounds curt on the phone. In her world, every minute she spends on the phone with you is a minute she won't get to spend on the phone with the media. However, out of sight is out of mind. You must strike a careful balance between falling out of your publicist's radar and hounding her, because neither results in coverage.

SEVEN QUESTIONS *NOT* TO ASK YOUR PUBLICIST

A savvy author is going to have a lot of questions about the publicity for his or her book. Yet there are some questions that are notorious for riling publicists. I list a few below, and reasons to avoid them. I encourage you to think of them as the seven deadly sins.

1. **"Have you tried Oprah? (or Larry King, Charlie Rose, Regis and Kelly, or Terry Gross)?"** Publicists know that these people's shows really sell books, and go for them before anything else if you and your book are even remotely appropriate. They're already under a lot of pressure to get you on these programs. They won't appreciate more.

2. **"Could you overnight a copy to . . . ?"** You're asking your publicist to stop what she's doing (perhaps preparing for a big marketing meeting where she'll discuss your book) and send a copy by the costliest means possible. If it's a *major* show or publication and they've expressed *real* and

urgent interest, by all means ask for this. Otherwise, just e-mail the info to your publicist and ask her to mail the book or send it via UPS Ground as soon as possible.

3. **"Anything new?"** If there were, your publicist would have told you; we're not shy about trumpeting success. Keep in mind that your publicist constantly hears this same question from her immediate supervisor, the publisher, the sales reps, the foreign rights department, the subrights department, and the editors. Then multiply the pestering by ten for the number of books she's working on, in some capacity, on any given day.

4. **"Did the host/reporter who just interviewed me even read the book?"** Unfortunately, the answer is, probably not. But please don't be offended. They may be even busier than your publicist. That's why she sent them press material to crib from.

5. **"Is (insert name of show or publication) going to do anything with my book?"** Your publicist will do her best to get a "yes" or "no" from each media outlet about your book, but she isn't always able to, and pushing the media for an answer when they haven't responded to a galley, a finished book, two e-mails, a fax, and three voice mail messages isn't going to help her reputation—or yours. Sometimes, no answer is an answer—if they were interested, they'd have called. Also keep in mind that when she does get a "no," your publicist might not get a reason or the reason may be vague ("it's just not right for our magazine," or "the host wasn't interested"). This is frustrating, but perfectly normal.

6. **"Could you send a copy to my friend Mandy from high school? She knows Katie Couric's assistant."** It's nice that your friend knows Katie Couric's assistant. However, your

publicist probably knows Andrea Smith, the books producer at the *Today Show* (who has been on the list of publishing's most powerful people) and the person there
who is most likely to actually do something with your
book—and chances are your publicist has sent your book
to her. Remember, your publicist only has so many copies
to send to the media. You don't want her to waste one,
and insisting that she send one to acquaintances of yours
who have *distant* connections to the media is a sure way to
do so. However, if you yourself have a direct connection
to the media (e.g., your friend Mandy from high school
is Katie Couric's assistant—or better yet, your friend from
high school is *Katie Couric*), then by all means ask your
publicist to send. She'll be grateful.

7. **"How many other books are you working on right
   now?"** More than you want to know about. Trust me.

THE PUBLICIST WITHIN THE ORGANIZATION

A publishing house can be a tough place for an author to navigate.
It's often hard to tell where one person's responsibilities end and
another person's begin (the lines between marketing and publicity
are particularly blurry). So, too, it's hard to tell who reports to
whom, and which employees interact on a regular basis. Your relationship with your publicist will be stronger if you understand her
role within the company.

In general, the publicity department is a subset, or offshoot, of
the marketing department. Publicity budgets are usually part of a
book's overall marketing dollars, and the director of publicity
often reports to the director of marketing (who tends to report
directly to the publisher). The entire publicity staff—or at least the
director of publicity—attends most marketing meetings. These

meeting are usually held on a weekly or biweekly basis and are an opportunity to discuss overall publishing issues as well as specific books. Generally, three to five imminently forthcoming or recently off-press titles are put on the agenda for each gathering so that they can be discussed in detail. Their editors usually attend, as do several members of the sales force and, sometimes, the publisher himself. When a publicist has a title on the docket, it's something of a tension-inducing experience for her. She has to provide a written recap of all of the media the book has received or been promised thus far (an awkward thing if there's little to report), and has to be prepared to give a verbal update on any media that has taken a pass as well as any media she is still pursuing. In other words, she's in the hot seat. So if your publicist doesn't return your call right away, meeting prep may be the reason.

There are many other ways your publicist works closely with the marketing department at both the planning and execution stage. Together, they will determine which cities, if any, you will be sent to and what you will do there in terms of events. They may present your book at sales conference together. They may collaborate on galley or ARC copy. Your book's marketing manager may look to its publicist for help determining when to run an ad so that it can time with media coverage, and may also ask the publicist to supply quotes from reviews that could be used in the ad. And the list goes on . . . and on . . . and on. Indeed, these departments are interdependent.

Your publicist also has close ties to your editor. Ideally, they have an open relationship in which the publicist can be honest about your book's media potential and your editor can be honest about what you bring to the table both in terms of the quality of your book and your personal promotability. Together, they can brainstorm places to approach and various ways to approach them. This kind of discourse at the start lays the groundwork for continued communication during the publicity process so that the editor is kept abreast of all goings-on without having to push for updates. It also makes it possible for a publicist to enlist the help of an editor should any problems arise—a disgruntled agent who steps out of bounds by contacting the publicist directly; an author who consistently forgets about her interviews; an op-ed piece that just won't come together; a string of really, really bad reviews.

That said, it's important for you to realize that, while your editor will always be there for you in a pinch, there does come a point where your publicist must become your point-person. The transition from editor to publicist should start to take place at the galley stage. If it doesn't, it will lead to bad feelings all around. A good editor will help facilitate this transition by setting up a meeting or phone call that involves all three of you—by "handing you over," as it were. But even an intro by e-mail will suffice. Regardless of how you do it, you have to "make the break." Failure to do so will jeopardize your cause.

There are two other departments with whom your publicist has a lot of interaction—subrights and sales. Subrights can be broken down into two main categories—international and domestic. And domestic can be broken down into five smaller categories—serial, paperback, audio, film and TV, and book club. Most facets of subrights rely heavily on publicity's results, and your publicist is likely to cc them on any e-mail that announces major hits so that they can use it to get more deals (and more lucrative ones at that). In turn, publicity can make use of subrights' accomplishments. A well-placed first serial excerpt, which runs pre-pub, can lead to other media interest and in effect help launch the book. Foreign rights, book club, and audio deals give the publicist more successes to trumpet to the media ("the book is being translated into a dozen languages," "it's a Book-of-the-Month Club selection," "James Earl Jones is doing the audio"), and a film or TV deal can lead to coverage in celebrity gossip columns and magazines like

Entertainment Weekly and *People*—in other words, places that may have otherwise ignored the book. For this reason, your publicist will appreciate any effort you make to let her know when you get this good news.

As for the sales force, expect your publicist to communicate regularly with the sales director, the sales managers who handle the national accounts (Barnes & Noble, Amazon.com, Borders, etc.), the individual reps who sell to the stores (whether they're specific to your publisher or employed by your publisher's distributor), and even the "special sales" force (people who sell to specialty and gift accounts like Restoration Hardware and Hallmark, as well as cataloguers like L. L. Bean). The collaboration will range from asking them for bookstore suggestions when planning a tour, to responding to their requests for copies of reviews so that they can share them with their buyers, to working with them to arrange for an author to appear at a regional trade show. They'll be cc'd on most media recaps, and they won't be shy about asking for one if they feel they need it.

So you see, your publicist is at the center of it all. She's the hub of the publishing wheel. And the stronger your relationship with her, the more she'll advocate on your book's behalf.

Chapter 6

The Tour and Author Events

Not every author gets a tour. Not every author should. For some books, it makes sense to send the author on the road. It's worth the publicist's time—and the publisher's money. For other books, it doesn't. And it isn't. And they won't.

What convinces a publicist that she should tour an author? She looks at a number of factors. Is it a "tour book," meaning is it the kind of book that lends itself to successful bookstore events? Novels and poetry fall into this category. (Who doesn't like to escape their own world for an hour? And poetry is so much better when it's *heard*.) So do biography, and history, and current affairs. (Who doesn't like an interesting talk?) Most self-help authors can't put bodies in chairs. (Public forums are tough for personal matters.) Same with business, and parenting, and health. Your publicist also assesses you to see if you're the kind of person who can magnetize a crowd. Will you glad-hand well and charm folks while you're signing? Are you someone whom the audience will line up just to meet? Finally, your publicist looks at the kind of media you could garner in each geographical market. Is it the kind of press you'd have to do face-to-face, in-studio, etc.? Or could you do it on the phone from your own hometown?

When an author is sent on tour, the number of cities can vary. It could range from a couple, to a dozen, to twenty-five. It could mean an event in every city, or it could mean media alone. Usually, the cities are scheduled consecutively (it's cheaper that way—no flights home to factor in) but sometimes the publicist purposefully breaks a tour up so that she has time to book more media in between trips. Most of the time, however, she does them all at once—more chance of making national bestseller lists that way.

THE GOAL OF THE TOUR

The goal of the tour is to sell books—to do media that sells books, to do events that sell books, to generate buzz that sells books, to get on bestseller lists (which sells more books). Have I mentioned that the goal of the tour is to sell books?

If you speak at a reputable bookstore—especially a reputable independent—or as part of a reputable series, your publicist may have one other goal . . . to get you on C-Span II's *Book TV.* The show frequently tapes author events and airs them in their entirety. They especially like nonfiction in the categories of history, current affairs, science, biography, and politics. This national television exposure can do wonders for your book in terms of sales and interest (watching others on *Book TV* can also be a great learning tool as you're prepping for your events—so tune in). On occasion, *Book TV* even tapes an in-studio radio interview if it's a major show like NPR's *Diane Rehm* or Milt Rosenberg's *Extension 720* show on Chicago's WGN.

It's a stretch to actually call it a goal of the tour, but publishers do like to send authors to certain stores to thank the booksellers that support their houses (in other words, bookstores that move their titles). For this reason, publicists are very strategic. While it's unlikely they would choose a store with a weak reading series over one with a strong series just because the former does a bigger volume of business for them, all things being equal, the store that buys more of her company's books would get the nod. So if they send you to San Francisco and place you at Cody's rather than Kepler's or Black Oak, or Book Passage rather than Stacey's or Books Inc., sales volume might be the reason. Also, your publicist may try to balance the number of independent stores with the number of chain stores.

HOW TO GET ON LOCAL BESTSELLER LISTS

Publicists try to get their touring authors on local bestseller lists. The key is to make sure the events are held at stores that report their sales to these lists or, if the events are held at other locations, that reporting stores sell at these venues (when a stores sells at an event that's not in its own store, it's referred to as an "off-site.") In order to find out if a particular store reports to a particular bestseller list, just look beneath the list where the reporting stores are named. Keep in mind that this only works for local lists; most national ones (*New York Times, Wall Street Journal, Business Week,* etc.) take great pains to keep their reporting stores a secret to guard against publisher tampering. Also, not all cities have these lists. Boston does. Los Angeles, Denver, and D.C., too. So does San Francisco (in fact, they have two—the *Chronicle* and the *East Bay Express*).

It takes a surprisingly few number of books sold to get on these local lists. In a slow week in pretty much any market, an event at which fifty to seventy-five copies are sold can be enough to garner the number nine or ten spot—and thus, the right to refer to your book as a "bestseller" in perpetuity.

PLANNING THE TOUR

When it comes to planning your tour, timing is crucial on two levels. First, you or your publicist need to secure your tour events far enough in advance to get the venues you want. Most bookstores schedule events three to four months in advance. Series at venues like museums (the Smithsonian in D.C., the Field in Chicago, the American Museum of Natural History in New York, the Museum of Nature and Science in Denver, etc.) and major libraries start to fill up at least six months ahead. Universities may book as much as a year in advance.

Second, timing is key in terms of when you do your tour. Most authors make the mistake of going on tour too soon after their book's on-sale date. You want to give both the media and the consumer time to hear about—and become intrigued by—your book. Therefore, I recommend you tour no sooner than one month after your book hits stores. This is contrary to the view held by many publicists who opt for starting the tour the minute the books hit stores. Personally, I think these immediate tours are a great way to guarantee your audience will consist of empty chairs.

When choosing your tour cities, look for ones with a blend of good media and good bookstores (which indicate a strong book-buying public). Also consider things like where you grew up and where the events described in your book take place. If you need to do the tour on the cheap, also think about cities where you have friends or family with whom you can stay.

Will you be traveling for work or pleasure shortly after your book comes out? If so, let your publicist know so that she can piggyback events on those visits.

WHAT TO EXPECT WHILE YOU'RE ON TOUR

When publishers agree to tour authors, there are certain things they'll pay for and certain things they won't. For starters, don't expect them to pay travel costs for your spouse, significant other, child, or dog (yes, I actually had an author request that once). Your publisher will pay for your airfare (or train fare, rental car, or bus). If you're used to traveling first-class and staying at five-star hotels, you're going to have to adjust to a coach fare and the Marriott or the Hyatt (if a first-class ticket is really an issue, ask your publicist if you can use your frequent-flyer miles to upgrade).

Your publisher will pay for your meals while you're on tour. Let me repeat that, *your* meals. If you brunch with your high school sweetheart or have dinner with your cousin, don't expect your publisher to foot that person's portion of the bill. Have a glass of wine, not a bottle. Have the chicken, not the filet mignon—or at least don't have the lobster. Avoid the fanciest restaurants, and only order room service if you're truly exhausted or your schedule necessitates it. Go light on the honor bar. Save receipts for cash expenses such as airport snacks and cabs, and send them to your publicist (with the amount totaled) as soon as the tour is over so she can get you reimbursed.

Some publishers provide their authors with a credit card in his or her own name. It can be used for all of the tour expenses, and the bill goes right to the publicist. While this is probably the easiest system for authors and publishers alike, realize that your publicist will no doubt scrutinize the bill and will have the right to deny reimbursement for any suspect charges. So if you don't want your publicist wondering exactly what movie you watched in your hotel room, it's best to avoid the pay-per-view. And while your manicure will look lovely while you're signing all those books, don't try to dupe your publisher into paying for it.

In some cities, you'll be responsible for getting yourself to and from your interviews and events. In others, your publisher may arrange a car service for you. If your schedule is tight, your publicist may hire an author escort. Author escorts are professional guides who get authors where they need to go. Usually, they pick you up at the airport or at your hotel. They'll troubleshoot for you along the way. If you're running behind for a radio or TV interview because your talk started late or your flight was delayed or you got stuck in traffic, they'll call ahead and warn the producer. If you pop a shirt button, they'll get needle and thread. If you need caffeine, they'll by all means provide it. In between your appointments, they may take you to area bookstores to sign stock (we call these "drop-bys"). Treat author escorts well and make use of their expertise. For example, they may know a particular reporter's pet peeves or a bookstore's little quirks.

If you're sending yourself on tour and want to hire an author escort, below is a list of some of the best. Keep in mind that they usually cost around $250 per day (which doesn't include gas, cell phone charges for calls they make on your behalf, etc.), but you'd spend almost as much (in some cities, more) just for a car service and wouldn't get the same kind of attention. The best way to get your money's worth: ask the escorts for their local media list. Most author escorts provide them free to their clients. Because they're based there, they usually have better contacts—and more of them—than your publicist, and their lists are really up-to-date. If your tour is extensive and you want to avoid having to do the legwork to locate an escort in each market, contact Emily Laisy at Promotion Network: (800) 861-1235. She has a stable of about 130 drivers nationwide, and charges around $225 per city.

Ken Wilson Media Services
(Los Angeles, California)
kwmedia@earthlink.net
(818) 760-2678

Jeff Silverman, Los Angeles Media Escort Services
(Los Angeles, California)
castorave@aol.com
(323) 782-3854

Sheryl Benezra-Tat, Media Works
(Los Angeles, California)
sbtmworks@aol.com
(323) 937-5885

Charles Morrell
(Los Angeles, California)
Aloha10243@aol.com
(760) 360-7274

David Golia, Golia Media Services
(San Francisco, California)
goliamedia@aol.com
(415) 656-1385

Naomi Epel, Naomi Epel & Associates
(San Francisco, California)
naomi@observationdeck.com

Lisa Maxson, Guidance Systems
(Boulder/Denver, Colorado)
(303) 455-0551

Joan Robbins Media Escort
(Southern Florida—Miami, Ft. Lauderdale,
Boca Raton, Palm Beach, Vero Beach)
joan@pagebuild.com
(305) 936-0141

Jane Fischbach, Inc.
(Atlanta, Georgia)
(404) 252-1761

Don Lynch, Chicago Media Tours
(Chicago, Illinois)
chgomedia@attbi.com
(773) 271-7785

Bill Young, Midwest Media
(Chicago, Illinois)
(708) 848-7501

Sally Carpenter, Guidance Systems of New England
(Boston, Massachusetts/Providence, Rhode Island)
(401) 245-1904

Isabel Keating, Around Town Agency
(Minneapolis/St. Paul, Minnesota)
isabellakeating@hotmail.com
(612) 473-3343

Halle Sadle, HMS Media Services
(Portland, Oregon)
hmsadle@aol.com
(503) 297-9636

Joan Mendel, Media Connections, Inc.
(Philadelphia, Pennsylvania)
jmmediacon@aol.com
(610) 667-7843

Charles Roberts Author Escort & Media Services
(Houston/Austin, Texas)
charles@authortours.net
(713) 629-1556
http://www.authortours.net

Joy Delf Media Services
(Seattle, Washington)
jdms@joydelf.com
(206) 525-0232

Helen Gibson and Gail DiRe, Xetera Media Services
(Seattle, Washington)
HGXetera@aol.com/gdire@juno.com
(206) 236-1909 / (425) 820-6829

Paul Peachey, Bookfame
(Washington, D.C./Baltimore, Maryland)
info@bookfame.com
(202) 544-3305
http://bookfame.com

Beverly Stein Halpern, Halpern Media
(Tennessee, Arkansas, Mississippi)
bshalp@aol.com
(901) 754-8143

So what is a typical tour day like? It may start rather early (e.g., 7:00 A.M.), perhaps with a phoner (a radio interview done by telephone) from your hotel room with a local radio station, or even a phoner with a station in the next town on your tour. At 7:30 your author escort picks you up and whisks you to a local radio station for a live, in-studio, drive-time interview at 8:00 A.M. Next, you head to the offices of the city's major newspaper for coffee with a reporter while he interviews you for a profile piece. That lasts from 9:00–10:00. Then it's off to a local TV station for a live, in-studio interview on their 11:00 A.M. news. After that, you hit two bookstores to sign stock before grabbing lunch. At 1:00 P.M., you're back in a radio studio taping a segment that will air the following week. By 2:15, you're in your hotel lobby sitting across from a freelancer who is interviewing you for a magazine article. You have time to swing by another bookstore before 4:00 when your media escort drops you off at the offices of a magazine for a meeting with their editor. During the conversation, you realize you haven't had a bathroom break since you left the hotel that morning. You wonder how many hours a person can "hold it" before it creates a bladder infection, but decide against asking the editor who, by the way, doesn't seem to have a piece by you, or about you, in mind. You get good face time with him though, and hope it'll lead to a topic (a week later, he calls and asks you to write an article about a topic that came up during the discussion; you do, and your book is mentioned in your bio line). By 5:30 you're back in your hotel with a sandwich your escort bought while you were at the magazine. You hit the bathroom (hurray!), down the sandwich, shower, and get dressed. The phone rings and it's your escort. She's in the lobby ready to take you to the bookstore where you're speaking. She reminds you to bring your bags, which she throws in her trunk. After your talk, you head to an autographing table. The local newspaper reporter who interviewed you earlier has sent over a photographer. He takes a handful of "candid" shots while you do your signing. You scrawl your name in the remaining stock. By then it's 8:15 and your escort has just enough time to get you to the airport to catch the last shuttle to New York so that you're set to repeat the process. When the alarm goes off at 6:00 A.M., you think of Bill Murray's movie *Groundhog Day* in which each morning is like the one before. Welcome to the wonderful world of touring.

TROUBLESHOOTING WHILE ON TOUR

One of the toughest tasks while on tour is to deal with last-minute changes to your itinerary. It's not unheard of for a publicist to receive an interview request or cancellation the day before an author is in town—or even the day of. Your publicist is going to need to be able to get in touch with you 24/7 to advise you of additions and subtractions to your schedule. Get in the habit of carrying a cell phone (and keeping it "on") and train yourself to always check for a message light on your hotel phone. Don't be surprised to find a fax waiting for you at the hotel's front desk upon your arrival.

If you have a radio or TV interview—especially a live one—and for some reason your media escort or driver doesn't show, just hail a taxi and get to the studio. Worry about what happened later (if possible, call your publicist from the cab so she can sort it out for you). The same holds true if you're giving a talk—you don't want to keep your audience waiting. Have your publicist's work, cell, and home phone numbers with you at all times and call her if there is any problem, even if it's to say, "I screwed up and over-slept." She won't want to hear it secondhand, believe me. And speaking of oversleeping, don't trust the hotel wake-up call. Invest in a decent travel alarm clock.

Should you miss a flight while on tour, call your publicist immediately. She'll try to get you on the next one. If it was the last flight out, she'll try to get you on the first one the following day. She may even explore alternate methods of transportation, like a train or rental car. If necessary, she will try to reschedule your media or see if you can do it by phone or from an affiliate studio in the city you're still in. I once had a VIP author who was giving an evening speech in Boston. It ran quite late, and by the time she made it to Logan the shuttle flights to La Guardia were done. She had to be in New York the next day for *Good Morning America* at 7:00 A.M. The solution: a car service. It cost $600—double the cost of the flight (for which I could not get a refund). But for a national morning show, I was willing to do it. And luckily, my author was willing to ride through the night. Another time, a colleague's author was supposed to fly from Los Angeles to San Francisco where he was to do Fox News's *O'Reilly Factor*—live. Because of L.A. traffic (he was from England and didn't know how bad it can be), he missed his flight. He called his publicist right away, and she was able to get in touch with the producer and have the interview moved from the San Francisco affiliate to the Los Angeles affiliate. Problem solved, though it did mean he had to hustle to San Fran after the show in order to make it to his event at Corte Madera's Book Passage on time.

I encourage my authors to carry a copy of their book with them to every radio interview just in case the host or producer has misplaced it. It's hard to read a passage from your book on air without a copy of your book in front of you. The same holds true for TV interviews. You want them to flash a shot of the book, which is hard to do if they can't find it.

To avoid wardrobe quandaries while on tour, aim for fabrics that travel well—trust me, you won't have time to iron.

TYPES OF EVENTS

Bookstores

Most authors want to give talks at tons of stores—everything from the Borders or Barnes & Noble around the corner to independents across the country that they've heard are prestigious (stores like Shaman Drum in Ann Arbor, Powell's in Portland, Books & Books outside of Miami, Prairie Lights in Iowa City, and Elliott Bay in Seattle). Sometimes, an event at one of these places is a great idea that leads to lots of sales. Other times, it leads to a disappointed author and a totally embarrassed bookstore. Events that fail also strain the publisher's relationship with the store, and make it hard for the publicist to book events in the future.

It's important to assess each bookstore's ability to host a successful event for your particular book. The best way to do this—hit the store's Web site. If yours is an adventure book and they've hosted Jon Krakauer, chances are they have ties to the kind of audience who would turn out for your event. It's also important to make sure they have a vibrant reading series. One tip-off—if they don't have a person who has the title "Events Coordinator" or "Community Relations Coordinator," events at their store are probably just an afterthought. That's not the kind of place you want to speak. Keep in mind that many bookstores have special reading series that complement their main one, some of which involve partnering up with a local organization or corporation. For example, University Bookstore in Seattle pairs up with the Harbor Club for a business book program. Tattered Cover in Denver works with the Land Library on a nature reading series. I encourage you to explore these opportunities. Such special series can be terrific because they draw a dedicated audience. It can mean a better turnout, and better word of mouth about the book after the event because it's a topic about which attendees are passionate. Also, don't be afraid to do an unusual event. Rakestraw Books outside of San Francisco recently hosted one of my authors, Sharman Apt Russell, for her book *An Obsession with Butterflies*. They held the event at noon in the lavish gardens of a local woman of considerable wealth. Though open to the general public, it was mostly attended by the woman's friends—the "ladies who lunch" who would rather die than miss a "social event." And let me tell you—those ladies buy books.

With a few notable exceptions (e.g., the Borders on Michigan Avenue in Chicago and the Barnes & Noble in Union Square in New York), I prefer to schedule my authors at independent book-stores rather than chains. It has been my experience that the indies put more effort behind event promotion. Also, they tend to know their community a little better, which enables them to select authors and books that will go over well. Mark Pearson—Events Director at Brookline Booksmith, a fabulous independent just out-side of Boston that does two or three author events each week—

sums it up well: "Our event choices reflect the personality of the store as well as the interests of our customers. Since chain events are handled at the management level, this is often not the case." In his eyes, the key to a good author event is "The right book at the right store. That's why we say no a lot."

When last I corresponded with him, Pearson had, in the same month, hosted Robert Stone (*Bay of Souls*), Bill Bryson (*A Short History of Nearly Everything*), Margaret Atwood (*Oryx and Crake*), Elizabeth Berg (*Say When*), and Sherman Alexie (*Ten Little Indians*). Not too shabby. Pearson books his events four to six months in advance, directly with authors as well as through publicists. He says he gives preference to local authors—"particularly friendly and talented ones." He is open to being approached using a variety of methods—phone, e-mail, fax, mail, in-person—but says "e-mail is great particularly when a press kit is attached. A twenty-minute verbal rundown of the plot on the phone is my least favorite." Pearson does like to see a galley before making his decision as to whether an author is right for his store. He says, "For me the actual work is more relevant than pedigree or publisher sloganeering. Galleys are also a useful tool for garnering on-the-floor bookseller buzz, something I consider a priority in the making of a successful event."

When asked what kinds of events work well for him, Pearson replied, "Fiction, all kinds of fiction." This is often the case. Novels—and even short story collections—have a way of drawing the customer to the store. Perhaps it's a throwback to our childhood; who doesn't have fond memories of having a story read to them by a parent or favorite teacher? Storytime for grown-ups—not a bad way to spend an evening.

To secure an event at an independent, all you or your publicist need to do is email or fax their events person a brief description of your book and your author bio, with information on when you'd be available to speak. If you've spoken at bookstores in the past, it's good to mention that. If your event would be part of a larger tour, mention that as well (it signals the events coordinator that yours is a big book).

The process for securing an event at a chain bookstore is similar, but instead of reaching out to the events coordinator at a particular store, it involves approaching the events person who handles your publisher nationally. That means a call to the Borders headquarters in Ann Arbor and the B&N offices in New York, even if you're looking to speak at stores in Philly and D.C. While this centralized method seems a bit odd, it actually works quite smoothly. However, these chain events coordinators prefer not to deal with authors directly. So ask your publicist to place the call.

Authors often ask me what they should do at their events. If you're a poet, novelist, short story writer, or children's book author, the answer is simple—read! A few brief comments in between poems is perfectly appropriate. A few words about where the idea for the story came from can be a nice way to start. If you're reading from a novel and the section is later in the book, you'll need to give background info on the plot and acquaint everyone with the characters. If yours is a work of nonfiction, it's not so cut and dry. The best nonfiction events tend to be informal lectures (meaning you have some notes to work from but don't bury your head in a prepared script). I particularly like it when nonfiction authors intersperse their talks with passages from their book. It gives the audience a feel for the prose, and leads, I think, to better sales. When asked whether he prefers authors to read from their book or just to talk about it, Pearson replied "I prefer a combo but think that an author should focus their presentation on what they do best—I've seen some folks read their own stuff as if they were reading it for the first time."

Charles Lago, Events Coordinator at San Diego's Current Events Bookstore, usually hosts six authors a week (he does best with works of nonfiction, especially books on current affairs and politics, and books by or about celebrities; he recently hosted Bill Maher and Carol Channing). He says, "I have found that people really like it when an author takes questions. My preference is for an author to speak on his/her book for about twenty to twenty-five minutes, then take questions. I'm not big on listening to an author read from their book. However, for fiction events that's a little different although you have to be careful not to lose the audience by reading lengthy passages."

For the most part, I advise my authors against using slides. They just seem kind of impersonal. Powerpoint slides are particularly deadly—they harken back to college or perhaps the corporate board. However, on occasion, a good old-fashioned slide show can be a lot of fun. One of my authors, Theresa Maggio, wrote a book about the mattanza, an ancient fishing ritual off the coast of Sicily. For a half-hour on a summer night at her Wordsworth talk in Cambridge, we got to view the fishermen, the nets they made, the spears they used, and those glossy, big-eyed, bluefin tuna—as big as any man! What an amazing night (though I'll never eat a tuna sandwich again).

If you're nervous about public speaking or concerned that you may not be able to draw a crowd as the sole attraction, consider doing your event as an "in conversation with." This is a format in which a local radio or TV personality, a local newspaper reporter, a local author, or some other local household name interviews you about your book in front of an audience. Picture two armchairs angled toward each other. It creates a relaxed atmosphere for you, and you're not up there "on stage" alone. The intimacy of this format is usually quite appreciated by attendees, and your interviewer's "fame" can help to lure more people to the store. If you like this idea, just talk to your publicist—or the store's events coordinator—about it. They can help you chose the right person and get them on board.

If the mere idea of a solo event makes your mouth go dry and your knees start to shake, there is one other option—a panel. Picture a long table with four or five chairs behind it and a mike in front of each. Now picture a moderator in one of those chairs, and the others filled by experts in your field or others who have written books. These events can be fascinating and lots of fun. They can also draw a crowd. The downside: if your panel is peppered with other authors plugging their books, it may compromise your sales.

If you're a poet or you write fiction and you're concerned about attendance, consider doing a dual event with someone who writes in your genre. Your publicist or the store's events coordinator can help you find someone perfect, or perhaps you have an author friend who would fit the bill.

In terms of event logistics, some authors like to stand at a podium, some just like a stool. If possible, let the bookstore know your preference before your arrival. Some stores can provide an armchair (especially good for children's books). If all they give you is a table and desk chair, I suggest you sit on the front of the table (otherwise, if you sit in the chair behind it, it creates a barrier between you and the audience).

Expect that you'll be microphoned. Most authors opt for a lavaliere mike (the kind that clips to your shirt), though sometimes all that's offered is the kind that's part of the podium. If you're not used to using a mike, get to the store a little early to practice. If the room is small enough and you can project, you can try it without a mike, provided there's not much background noise (the voices of customers roaming the store, clanging cash registers, ringing phones, and all the other dear sounds of a bookstore). Also be on the lookout for noisy heat or air-conditioning units.

What else should you expect during your bookstore event? For starters, keep in mind that not all bookstore events actually take place in bookstores. For example, Globe Corner—a wonderful travel bookstore in Cambridge—does all its events down the street at the First Parish Church. Similarly its fellow Cambridge haunt, Harvard Bookstore, holds many events on campus in the Sackler Auditorium. Ruminator Books in St. Paul holds its larger events at Macalester College. So, rule number one is to make sure you know where you're going!

There are a number of quirky things that can happen during a bookstore event, and handling them gracefully is absolutely key. No one wants to buy a book by a jerk! So if the store employee who gives your introduction doesn't know how to pronounce your name, don't interrupt to correct them. When it's your turn, simply say "Hi, I'm [insert name]. Thanks for coming this evening." The audience will then know the proper way to say your name. Same thing goes if he screws up the title. Also, if the person giving your introduction clearly hasn't read your book and is lifting the description straight from the flap copy, don't make a big deal of it.

It's rare that authors have to deal with hecklers, but should one make himself known—and should it become impossible to ignore him—simply announce that you'll be happy to continue once that person is removed. The events coordinator or store manager should then see to it that the heckler is escorted out. Apologize for the interruption (even though, of course, it wasn't your fault) and resume your talk. If you had been reading, go back a paragraph or two so that your listeners can ease back in. Try to maintain your composure. Remember, it could be worse: one author speaking for Harvard Bookstore actually got a pie in the face.

When your talk and/or reading is done (usually twenty-five to thirty minutes), it's time for Q&A. Let the audience know you'd welcome their questions and call on them as they raise their hands. If the audience is really packed in, and if there are a lot of hands up, it's helpful if, in addition to pointing or gesturing to the person on whom you're calling, you describe them briefly: "the lady in the red shirt," "the gentleman standing next to the plant." This avoids confusion and that awkward "no, you go," "oh please, I insist."

Audience questions are often wonderfully insightful. They can also be quite strange. Sometimes they're inappropriately personal, asking you to reveal too much or revealing too much themselves. All you can do is be tactful. "You know, I've never thought of that. Hmm . . ." is a perfectly fine response, as is "Wow, that must be tough. I wish I had an answer for you." If a question is clearly antagonistic, or hurtful, or insulting, just say, "I won't be answering that," and call on the next raised hand.

Every author has to deal with chatty autograph seekers and quasi-rabid fans—ones who hold up the booksigning line and monopolize your time. If you're lucky, the events coordinator or another store representative will come to your rescue. If necessary, you can say something like "It's been fun talking with you. Sorry to have to keep things moving," or "Great to get to meet you. I guess I'd better circulate."

If there are extra copies of your book after you're done signing, it's time for the oldest trick in the book (no pun intended): offer to autograph them. A copy signed by you is a copy the store cannot return. And, stores will often put a special sticker on the book to let people know it's signed (which helps it sell). Sometimes, they'll even create a display with the autographed copies. When asked what he does with the leftover autographed books, Pearson responded, "Bonfire." But then he remembered his comments would be shared with the public, and added, "Or we display autographed copies for about six weeks after the event."

Take advantage of your time at the store to get to know the booksellers. Ask how long they've worked there. Ask them what they're reading. Avoid the "hard-sell," but if through your own peculiar charm you can convince them to evangelize your book, it can lead to far greater sales. In Pearson's words, when an author makes a lasting (favorable) impression, "It always leads to book-seller buzz, which beats out media plugs and critical kudos when it comes to sales on the floor."

Despite valiant efforts, turnout at author events is sometimes very low. It's hard to know how few is too few to speak to, but generally, I'd say if there are at least five people, you really ought to proceed. Fewer than that and the best solution: adjourn to the local bar. They'll be delighted to get you one-on-one, and you, my friend, will need a drink in which to drown your sorrows. Just remember—it *happens*. Bad weather, good weather, holidays, and conflicting events—literary and otherwise—can wreak havoc on attendance. It doesn't necessarily have anything to do with your book.

The opposite can also happen—an event where the turnout is higher than expected. Depending on the store's fire code, guests may be able to squeeze in by sitting on the floor, standing up in the back of the room, etc. This may make the room uncomfortably hot, so you might want to shorten your talk a bit. If, due to a larger than expected crowd, the store runs out of books, ask them if they have bookplates (little stickers you can sign that the reader can affix to your book's title page once they get a copy). You can even have some printed beforehand and carry them with you just in case (they're always nicer than the store's since they can be customized for your book).

It's a good idea to ask your publicist to call ahead a few days before your event to make sure the store's order of books arrived (she may pawn it off on your author escort or somebody in sales). In the unlikely event that it's the day of your event and no books are there to be found, your publicist or author escort may be able to talk your host into finding a nearby store that stocks your book, and borrowing copies from them. One last tip: if your event is within driving distance from your house, throw a box of books in the trunk. The Boy Scout motto is the touring author's best friend: "Always be prepared."

While bookstores are important, there are several other types of non-bookstore event venues—universities, libraries, book fairs and festivals, and reading series—that can lead to great sales for your book. There are added benefits to doing these kinds of events. For example, if you speak at a university, they'll poster the campus for you. If you speak at a book fair or festival, you'll be included in their promotional brochures—which often mail to thousands of people—and on their Web site. All of this amounts to free advertising. And if any of these venues will pay to bring you to their city, it amounts to a free trip during which you can do local media and bookstore drop-bys.

Libraries

If you live in a small town, ask your local library to host an event for you. They might even spring for a wine and cheese reception after. If you live in or will be traveling to a big city, try to get a spot in their library's lecture series. The New York Public Library, Chicago Public Library, and Boston Public Library are particularly great venues, and they partner with local bookstores so that books can be sold at the events.

Book Fairs and Festivals

Most book fairs and festivals take place during the Spring or Fall. These celebrations of the written word are open to the general public in terms of audience attendance, but in order to be a speaker/reader (on a panel or solo), you have to go through a selection process.

Following is a list of some of the best of these events, broken down by region.

New England

Boston Globe Book Festival
(Boston, Massachusetts)
(617) 929-2641

Concord Festival of Authors
(Concord, Massachusetts)
(978) 371-3167

Mid-Atlantic

Multicultural Children's Book Festival
(Washington, D.C.)
http://www.kennedy-center.org/programs/
specialprograms/bookfestival/
(202) 467-4600

National Book Festival
(Washington, D.C.)
http://www.loc.gov/bookfest
(888) 714-4696

National Press Club Book Fair and Authors' Night
(Washington, D.C.)
http://npc.press.org/programs/authorevents.cfm
(202) 662-7564

Delaware Authors Day
(Dover, Delaware)
http://www.state.de.us/heritage/authors.htm
(302) 577-5044

Baltimore Book Festival
(Baltimore, Maryland)
http://www.baltimoreevents.org/calendar/events/
book_index.html
(888) BALTIMORE

New York Is Book Country
(New York, New York)
http://www.nyisbookcountry.com
(646) 557-6361

Rochester Children's Book Festival
(Rochester, New York)
http://www.footprintpress.com/
childrensbookfestival.htm
(585) 637-2260

Virginia Festival of the Book
(Charlottesville, Virginia)
http://www.vabook.org
(434) 924-3296

Fall for the Book Literary Festival
(Fairfax, Virginia)
http://www.fallforthebook.org
(703) 993-3986

Newport News Celebrates the Book
(Newport News, Virginia)
http://www.newport-news.va.us/library
(757) 926-8506

Hampton Roads African Heritage Book Expo
(Norfolk, Virginia)
http://www.blackwordsonline.com
(757) 547-5542

South

Book Island Festival
(Amelia Island, Florida)
http://www.bookisland.org
(904) 491-8176

Lee County Reading Festival
(Fort Myers, Florida)
http://www.lee-county.com/library/
ReadingFestival2003.htm
(239) 479-4636

Miami Book Fair International
(Miami, Florida)
http://www.miamibookfair.com
(305) 237-3258

Sarasota Reading Festival
(Sarasota, Florida)
http://www.sarasotareadingfestival.com
(941) 906-1733

St. Petersburg Times Festival of Reading
(St. Petersburg, Florida)
http://www.festivalofreading.com
(727) 892-2358

Atlanta Literary Festival
(Atlanta, Georgia)
http://www.atlantaliteraryfestival.com
(404) 259-4841

Southern Kentucky Festival of Books
(Bowling Green, Kentucky)
http://www.sokybookfest.org
(270) 745-5016

Kentucky Book Fair
(Frankfort, Kentucky)
http://www.kybookfair.com/kybookfair.htm
(502) 564-8300, ext. 297

Louisiana Book Festival
(Baton Rouge, Louisiana)
http://lbf.state.lib.la.us
(225) 219-9503

Tennessee Williams/New Orleans Literary Festival
(New Orleans, Louisiana)
http://www.tennesseewilliams.net
(504) 581-1144

USM Children's Book Festival
(Hattiesburg, Mississippi)
http://www.usm.edu/slis/bookfest.htm

North Carolina Literary Festival
(Chapel Hill, Durham, and Raleigh North Carolina)
http://www.lib.unc.edu/NClitfest

Novello Festival of Reading
(Charlotte, North Carolina)
http://www.novellofestival.net
(704) 336-2074

South Carolina Book Festival
(Columbia, South Carolina)
http://www.schumanities.org/bookfestival.htm
(803) 771-2477

Southern Festival of Books
(Nashville, Tennessee)
http://www.tn-humanities.org/sfbmain.htm
(615) 320-7001, ext. 15

West Virginia Book Festival
(Charleston, West Virginia)
http://www.wvhumanities.org/bookfest/
bookfest2.htm
(304) 343-4646

Ohio River Festival of Books
(Huntington, West Virginia)
http://www.ohioriverbooks.org
(304) 528-5700

Midwest

Midwest Literary Festival
(Aurora, Illinois)
http://www.midwestliteraryfestival.com
(630) 897-5500

Chicago Book Festival
(Chicago, Illinois)
http://www.chipublib.org/003cpl/cbf/CBF.Html
(312) 747-4300

Printers Row Book Fair
(Chicago, Illinois)
http://www.chicagotribune.com/extras/printersrow
(312) 222-3986

Twin Cities Book Festival
(Minneapolis, Minnesota)
http://www.raintaxi.com/bookfest
(612) 825-1528

Buckeye Book Fair
(Wooster, Ohio)
http://www.buckeyebookfair.com
(330) 262-3244

Wisconsin Book Festival
(Madison, Wisconsin)
http://www.wisconsinbookfestival.org
(608) 262-0706

Mountains and Plains

Rocky Mountain Book Festival
(Denver, Colorado)
http://www.aclin.org/~ccftb/fest_2001.htm
(303) 839-8320

Log Cabin BookFest
(Boise, Idaho)
http://www.logcablit.org
(208) 331-8000

High Plains Bookfest
(Billings, Montana)
http://www.downtownbilings.com/PARTNERSHIP/
bcpartners/bookfest/files/other.htm
(406) 248-1685

Montana Festival of the Book
(Missoula, Montana)
http://www.bookfest-mt.org
(406) 243-6022

Nebraska Book Festival
(Grand Island, Nebraska)
http://www.stuhrmuseum.org/book.htm
(308) 384-6209

Celebration of Books
(Tulsa, Oklahoma)
http://poetsandwriters.okstate.edu/celebration
(918) 594-8215

Great Salt Lake Book Festival
(Salt Lake City, Utah)
http://www.utahhumanities.org
(801) 359-9670

Southwest

Northern Arizona Book Festival
(Flagstaff, Arizona)
http://www.flagstaffcentral.com/bookfest
(928) 774-9118

Arizona Book Festival
(Phoenix, Arizona)
http://www.azbookfestival.org
(602) 257-0335, ext. 28

Vegas Valley Book Festival
(Las Vegas, Nevada)
http://www.vegasvalleybookfest.org
(702) 895-1878

Border Book Festival
(Mesilla, New Mexico)
http://borderbookfestival.org
(505) 524-1499

Santa Fe Festival of the Book
(Santa Fe, New Mexico)
http://www.santafelibraryfriends.org
(505) 955-4866

West Texas Book and Author Festival
(Abilene, Texas)
http://www.abilenetx.com/apl/festivalindex.html
(325) 793-4682

Texas Book Festival
(Austin, Texas)
http://www.texasbookfestival.org
(512) 477-4055

**San Antonio Inter-American Bookfair
& Literary Festival**
(San Antonio, Texas)
http://www.guadalupeculturalarts.org
(210) 271-3151

West Coast

Los Angeles Times Festival of Books
(Los Angeles, California)
http://www.latimes.com/extras/festivalofbooks
(800) LATIMES

Central Coast Book and Author Festival
(San Luis Obispo, California)
http://www.ccbookfest.org
(805) 546-1392

Pacific Northwest

Bumbershoot Literary Arts Festival
(Seattle, Washington)
http://www.bumbershoot.org
(206) 281-7788

Northwest Bookfest
(Seattle, Washington)
http://www.nwbookfest.org
(206) 378-1883

Canada

Banff Mountain Book Festival
(Banff, Alberta, Canada)
http://www.banffmountainfestivals.ca
(800) 413-8368

Multi-City

Latino Book and Family Festival
(Los Angeles, California; San Bernardino/
Riverside, California, and Chicago, Illinois)
http://www.latinobookfestival.com
(760) 434-7474

Reading / Lecture Series

A number of prominent and fabled institutions across the country have well-established reading and lecture series. An event at places like New York's 92nd Street Y or KGB Bar or Explorers Club, Palm Beach's Forum Club, San Francisco's Commonwealth Club, Chicago's Union League Club, and D.C.'s National Press Club or National Geographic Society can generate great sales. Even Minneapolis's Mall of America has authors speak in their rotunda on occasion. Across the river in St. Paul, Minnesota Public Radio hosts a well-known series called "Talking Volumes." There are tons of similar venues—cultural centers, museums, etc.—so hit the Web, ask around, and do your best to find them. Books can be sold by the institution's gift shop or by a local bookstore with whom they partner up. Note that these series rarely offer an honorarium and usually can't pay for travel or hotel expenses. So if you want to do this type of event and it's in another city, try to tie it into your tour or piggyback it with personal travel.

And if you're a Jewish author, don't ignore the JCCs (Jewish Community Centers). Many of them have excellent series and some even have author festivals.

Universities

Universities—as well as colleges and community colleges—frequently invite authors to give readings and talks. Sometimes they're just to classes, which doesn't do much in the way of sales (students can rarely afford to buy books they don't have to use in a course). However, sometimes they're part of a series that's open to students, faculty, and the community at large. In this case, you may receive an honorarium and the school may be willing to cover your costs. The university bookstore usually sets up a table outside the event so that you can sign when you're done speaking. To gain an invite to give such a talk, contact the English department if yours is a book of fiction or poetry. If yours is a work of nonfiction, contact the department that relates most closely to your subject matter, be it history, science, psychology, or what have you.

HOW TO PROMOTE EVENTS

In order to draw a crowd to each event, someone needs to get the word out to the public. Bookstores can promote author events in several different ways: easel-backs (which are small posters that can be displayed on a bookstore counter; they're mounted on foam board with a cardboard brace on the back), bagstuffers (flyers that get slipped in with every purchase), newsletter and Web site mentions, postcard mailings and e-mail blasts, listings in the calendar sections of local papers (and sometimes even ads in their "Books" sections), and PSAs (public service announcements) on local radio stations.

"Our Web site has become the best tool," explains Charles Lago of Current Events Bookstore. "We get a lot of hits weekly and we know people have bookmarked the site and visit regularly. Unlike many bookstores we update our site as soon as an event is confirmed. That way we get maximum publicity. We also produce a monthly newsletter. We highlight two of our signings monthly and list all the rest with detailed descriptions. We advertise some of our events in the book section of our daily, the *San Diego Union Tribune*, as well as the two weekly alternative papers, *The Reader* and *City Beat*. The most important thing is media coverage. An article in a main newspaper is invaluable and worth the effort it takes to get it. I also announce upcoming events at our signings especially when we have a large crowd."

While some stores are very aggressive and cover all the event pro- motion bases, other stores just manage to do the basics—if you're lucky. Your publicist may be willing to push the store a little to make sure they're doing all that they can do. However, she'll undoubtedly be busy trying to get media to interview you prior to the event and mention it—and perhaps even attend it. Therefore, I suggest you reach out to the store. Offer to supply them with addresses (e-mail or snail mail) of people you know in the area. If necessary, contact these folks yourself. You can also help by researching and contacting local organizations that might co-sponsor your event or at least encourage their members to attend. Offer to e-mail them a flyer that they can post in the lunchroom (or, better yet, send them enough for each employee's mailbox). Perhaps their director would even want to introduce you at the event.

When asked what an author can do to help a bookstore promote his or her event, Brookline Booksmith's Mark Pearson replied, "A mailing list always helps. Post fliers guerrilla style. Drop into the store: wooing booksellers with a dazzling personality is a great idea, acting self-important and entitled isn't." As for what he does in terms of promotion, Pearson says, "For all events: press releases to all local media outlets and events calendars, in-store display, window display, monthly calendars, quarterly newsletter, events page on our Web site, e-mail newsletter, fliers, mailings (if mailing list is included). Occasional display ad in *Boston Phoenix* or *Improper Bostonian* generally based on available co-op funds." (Note: co-op funds are dollars provided by the publisher to support the event; they're usually based on the amount of business the store did with that particular publisher the previous year.)

Many of these methods will also work for talks at libraries, universities, museums, etc. Regardless of where your event is being held, it takes a lot of effort—and not a little luck—to generate a decent crowd. And keep in mind that, while events can generate tons of buzz and lead to lots of future sales, only about ten percent of the people who attend your talk will plunk down the money for your book on the spot.

Chapter 7

Frequently Asked Questions

On July 25th, 2002, the headline of Martin Arnold's *New York Times* "Making Books" column read "Why the Writer Is Last to Know." The article listed some of the things authors always want to learn but have trouble finding out—chief among them, the promotional budget for their book. I don't advise that you push for this number. Efforts to get it are rarely successful and usually create bad blood (unless your contract specifies that your publisher spend a certain amount on promotion, your publisher isn't obligated to share the figure with you—and probably won't, lest it not meet with your approval). But first-time authors and seasoned authors alike have a lot of other publishing questions that can and should be answered—some specific to their book; many of them general.

Often, your attempts to get your questions answered will be met with a puzzling silence. This may be because you're asking the wrong person, so in the following FAQ I try to direct you to the most appropriate contact—be it your publicist, your book's marketing manager, your editor, or your agent. It may also be because the person you're asking is swamped (most publishing houses have a rather "streamlined" staff), or because, frankly, they get tired of answering the same questions for author after author.

If your question isn't answered in this chapter or elsewhere in this book, and if your first attempts to get an answer don't pan out, I urge you to keep trying, *provided* it's a question that could make a difference to your book's success. If you're just trying to satisfy your curiosity, you might be better off letting it drop.

This chapter documents some of the most frequently asked questions I receive—especially from first-time authors—and answers them with candor. For your convenience, I've broken the most frequently asked questions into four sections: Questions About the Media, Questions About Bookselling, Questions For or About Your Publicist, and Miscellaneous Questions.

QUESTIONS ABOUT THE MEDIA

Q: Is it okay to approach the media directly about my book?

A: The sad truth is that most editors, reporters, and producers do not like to be approached by authors directly. Some of them will humor you. Many of them will be rude to your face or hang up on you. Even if they take the bait and decide to interview you, your book is less likely to get a mention if you approach the media directly (they'll just use you for your expertise; if the publicist books it, they'll feel like they owe her a mention of the book). So it's far better for you to let your in-house or freelance publicist approach the media on your behalf. If you have a specific pitch idea, type it up for your publicist so that she can forward it to the media as her own if she sees fit. If you don't have a publicist but you have a good idea and a good working knowledge of the show or publication, then you can certainly give it a try . . . but consider yourself forewarned and by all means do tread lightly.

Q: How can I get copies of my reviews?

A: Your publicist probably subscribes to a clipping service such as Luce or Burrelle's. They scan thousands of newspapers, magazines, and Web sites looking for words or phrases that they've been asked by their clients to watch for—in this case, the name of your book. However, it can take these services two to three weeks to get the clip to the publicist. Most publicists mail the clips to the author (rather than fax them), so factor in another week before it gets to you. Your publicist may on occasion e-mail links to you, but if you're anxious to get a particular clip, it's best to try the newsstand or look online yourself.

Q: Some of the interviews I've been doing have only tangentially been about my book. Are they really worth doing?
A: Often the best way to get the media to bite is to peg your book to current events. Even if the resulting coverage doesn't relate directly to your book, it's a chance for people to hear your voice or see your name in print, and it's another opportunity for your book to be mentioned. That's reason enough to do it. Most people have to hear about a book a number of times before they'll purchase it. In publicity as in advertising, repetition is key.

Q: What do I do if I've had a bad interview?
A: Tell your publicist. If the interview was bad because the host was unprepared or hostile, at least she'll know not to schedule other authors for interviews with him. If it was a taped interview with a radio or TV show and it was really disastrous, she can ask them to re-tape it or kill it altogether. If it was an interview for a print publication, she can call to clarify things you may have misstated or even try to schedule a follow-up interview so that you can clarify them yourself. In some cases, if asked, reporters may be willing to show you (or her) the article before it runs so that corrections can be made. However, according to Anneli Rufus, Book Review Editor of San Francisco's *East Bay Express* where she does five or six author interviews a month, "Showing copy to interview subjects prior to publication, and letting them edit, is generally not done, though some interviewees request it. My paper has a rule against it. You can see the logic in that—whose article is it, anyway? We try to get facts right, of course, but the way to do that isn't to show it to the subject.

Sometimes I'll call or e-mail a subject after the interview if I'm looking over my notes and something is unclear." So, unless you have reason to suspect that the reporter has some truly ominous hidden agenda—e.g., to destroy your career—I recommend against asking for a pre-pub peek. No sense setting off alarm bells that might just make the reporter dig deeper or mention, in the article, that you might have something to hide.

One last thing about bad interviews: remember that, in the words of Rufus, "Doing interviews is a bit like dating in that chemistry means so much." So don't beat yourself up just because you and the reporter or host didn't click.

Q: What do I do if I get a bad review?
A: Try to remember that even though it's in a public forum it's just one person's opinion and that book critics, while for the most part quite professional, have their share of bad days and sometimes take them out on someone else (you) or something else (your book). If the particular reviewer to whom your book was assigned locked his keys in the car that morning or woke to the sound of his cat dislodging a hairball on his bed, you could be in for a doozie of a review and that's just the way it goes. So don't throw in the towel. It's perfectly normal for a very good book to get one (or two, or three) negative reviews. If the review was slightly inaccurate but you feel the error needs to be corrected, you can ask your publicist to request that the publication run a correction. An example would be if they botched the title of the book. If the review was grossly inaccurate (e.g., it said your book is against the First Amendment and it's clearly in favor of it), craft a letter to the editor and send it for publication. Be sure to run it by your publicist first. Keep in mind that the tone should be measured, not angry or defensive. And if you're the "make lemonade out of lemons" type, read the review again and see if there's *anything* quotable in it—even a couple of

lukewarm lines that cobbled together sound halfway good. If so, you can take delight in having your publicist post the snippet on Amazon.com. No better way to get back at the reviewer than to use his words to help you sell your book.

Q: What do I do if I'm approached by the media directly?
A: This is a hard one. My instinct is to say refer them to your publicist, who could make sure it's a legitimate opportunity and that it won't conflict with other media that has been solidified or that she's trying to solidify (and I'm not just talking about a scheduling conflict; there are some shows and publications that won't cover you if their competition does). However, if the reporter is on deadline or the producer is pressing you for a commitment, forwarding them to your publicist could jeopardize the booking because they might opt for another author or expert from whom they can get a quick "yes." So use your best judgment. And if you do decide to handle it yourself right then and there, be sure to notify your publicist as soon as possible so that she can e-mail press material to the media contact and get a book right off to them. That will increase the chances that they'll mention the book on air or in print.

Q: What does it mean when my publicist says I'm "over-exposed?"
A: "Over-exposed" is a term the media uses as a reason not to cover you or your book. It's rare, but it happens. It could be because of all the coverage you got for a previous book (especially if it's recent, and especially if its topic is similar to your new book). Or it could be that a reporter, editor, or producer feels this book has already been well covered (in other words, they feel they've been "scooped").

Q: What if I think a portion of my book is appropriate for excerpt in a newspaper or magazine—or even on the Web?
A: Most publishing companies have a subrights department which

seeks to secure such placements. Ask your publicist for the name of the subrights person who is handling first- and second-serial publication rights for your book (first-serial excerpts run pre-pub; second run after your book's publication date) and give them a call to see what their plans are. They might really welcome your suggestions for specific chapters that stand alone well and would appeal to particular publications. And they'll be glad to know you'd be willing to work with an interested magazine to tailor a selection to meet their needs by adding an intro, bridges between sections, etc.

Q: How do I go about becoming a syndicated newspaper columnist?
A: This is something most authors have to try to broker for themselves (or have their agent broker for them). Some of the best syndicates include:

> *Los Angeles Times* Syndicate
> King Features Syndicate
> Universal Press Syndicate
> *New York Times* Syndicate (which boasts such notables as pediatrician T. Berry Brazelton)

Many companies that syndicate are struggling right now because lots of papers won't pay for their content (instead choosing to fill their pages with articles written by staffers). Blame it on the economy. What most newspaper syndicates look for—more so than big name experts to pen columns—are writers who already have a client list of twenty-five or thirty . . . meaning writers whose column is already picked up by twenty-five or thirty papers. And the only way to get that is for the writer to approach each paper directly, which is, admittedly, rather labor intensive. Another possibility is to approach a smaller syndicate or consortium of publications. For example, United Parenting Publications, the parent company of

Boston Parents' Paper and about twenty-five other regional parenting papers, doesn't get as many eyeballs as the big syndicates, but they do reach a targeted audience of moms and dads.

Q: How can I get a regular column in a magazine?

A: The best thing to do is to write a lot of articles for the desired magazine on a freelance basis, then propose a steady gig. It gives them a chance to see that you're dependable (meaning you turn solid stories in on time) and that you have good ideas (and plenty of them).

Q: Should I hold a press conference about my book? Should I ask my publicist to hold one?

A: Probably not and probably not. Few books require these. In the past decade, I've hosted *one*—and, as it turns out, it was completely unnecessary. The best reason to host a press conference about your book is if you are a celebrity (and can be reasonably sure, therefore, that the media will show and take lots of photos). The second best reason is if your book divulges startling info. Figured out who Deepthroat is? Know where Hoffa's buried? If so, write the book—and hold a conference for it.

QUESTIONS ABOUT BOOKSELLING

Q: How does my book get sold to bookstores?

A: For the chain bookstores (Barnes & Noble, Borders, etc.), a national accounts rep employed by your publisher will present your book to the appropriate national buyer (each buyer is responsible for certain subjects, such as biography, business, reference, science, or fiction, for the entire chain) many months in advance of its release. Sometimes, a national accounts rep will arrange for an author to have coffee or lunch with the appropriate buyer just to get him extra interested in the book. This is a good thing for you to push for with your book's marketing manager, who can encourage the national accounts rep to arrange it. The chain decides on its own how to apportion the books to its various stores. For the independent bookstores, a regional sales rep will visit them in-person to present your book, along with all of the other books that are on your publisher's same list. There are too many independent bookstores in the United States for you to meet with the buyers at all of them, but the next best thing is for you to meet with your publisher's regional sales reps who can evangelize your book to them. And the best way to accomplish this is to speak at your publisher's sales conference. A sales conference is a gathering that occurs two or three times a year at which the publisher presents its entire list of books for a particular season or catalogue. It's a chance for the sales reps to become knowledgeable about the books so that they can go out and sell them to their accounts. Ask your book's marketing manager whether speaking at sales conference is a possibility. When we published a book called *Mean Genes*, the authors not only attended the sales conference at which their book was presented, but held a raffle at it—one in which they gave $1,000 of their own money to the winning rep. You can bet the reps—especially the one who took home a thousand bucks—sold the heck out of their book.

Q: How will bookstores find out about the media my book gets?
A: Ideally, your publicist will notify your book's marketing manager of important coverage, and will provide him with copies of key reviews and feature articles. The marketing manager will, in turn, pass this info along to the sales reps, who will pass it on to the bookstores. However, at least for the independent bookstores, it never hurts for you to let them know directly by faxing, mailing, or e-mailing them (calling is risky; they're often too swamped).

But only do so when you're receiving significant national coverage, or coverage in a major publication or station that's local to
the store. For example, if you're being profiled in the *Chicago Tribune*,
let Barbara's Books and Seminary Coop know. If your book is being
reviewed in the *Seattle Times*, tell Third Place Books and Elliott Bay. If
you're appearing on Denver's NPR affiliate, alert Tattered Cover and
Boulder Books. Try to give the heads-up in advance of the coverage
so stock can be ready and staff is prepared, but when it's print coverage, also provide them with a copy of the piece after it runs. They
may post the review or article in the store, which can lead to additional sales.

**Q: How can I get quotes from reviews on the Amazon.com page
for my book, and what does my Amazon ranking really mean?**
A: Good that you're thinking about this. When shopping on
Amazon, people do read these quotes. So it is important to post
them—and promptly. Your publicist can submit the quotes for you,
and you can help her out by typing them up and emailing them to
her. Keep in mind that there's a twenty-word maximum per quote,
and that you need to include the name of the publication and the
date the coverage appeared. Expect it to take two to three weeks for
the quotes to post once submitted. You can find out more about
the quotes process at http://www.amazon.com/exec/obidos/tg/
catalog-guide/guide/-/422230/103-5296917-1372617.

As for the rankings, when there's a major jump, it's a good indication that some big media has hit and been effective. But it's not
indicative of the number of copies you've actually sold. Here's how
Amazon explains it on their Web site (http://www.amazon.com/
exec/obidos/tg/catalog-guide/guide/-/406132/103-5296917-
1372617): "As an added service for customers, authors, and publishers, we want to show how items in our catalog are selling in
relation to one another. This bestseller list is much like the *New York*

Times bestseller list, except instead of listing just the top 50 or so titles, it lists more than two million! The lower the number, the higher the popularity for that particular title in comparison to other items listed. The calculation for a book's sales rank is based on Amazon.com sales and is updated regularly. The top 10,000 best sellers are updated each hour to reflect sales over the preceding twenty-four hours. The next 100,000 are updated daily. The rest of the list is updated weekly, based on several different factors."

Keep in mind that Amazon is not the authoritative resource for how your book is doing saleswise. It's just one of many accounts. For certain books (health titles because many people prefer to shop for them in their privacy of their home; technology titles because their Web-savvy readers tend to make their purchases online), it's a key one to be sure. But for other types of books, it's simply not as crucial.

Q: Why haven't any readers posted reviews of my book on Amazon.com?

A: In part, because you haven't asked any to. True, many of the Amazon reader reviews just happen. But it's important for you to ask friends, family members (with different last names than yours, of course), and colleagues to post reviews. Don't be shy about asking; lots of people are happy to help in this way. Also, when you get fan mail from readers, write them back and tell them you liked their comments, and ask them to post them on Amazon.com. They'll be tickled that you responded, and honored that you asked.

Q: What if a negative reader review is posted on Amazon.com? Can it be removed? It's affecting my rating.

A: Probably not. At least, not unless you can prove the author of the review has a personal vendetta against you. However, you can help yourself out by rallying your friends. If they submit positive reviews, you'll be back up to five stars in no time. Plus, since the most recent reviews are posted on top, they can knock the negative review down to the point where it can't be read without a lot of clicking and scrolling.

Q: How can I find out how my book is selling?
A: Your publisher should receive weekly reports from Amazon, Borders, B&N, and Walden, and should be willing to share them with you. They may also get data from a service called Bookscan. The best person to ask for this info—your book's marketing manager. Incidentally, that's also the person to ask about the ad campaign for your book, the direct-mail campaign for your book, etc. Your editor may also be able to provide you with the sales figures. Just be sure not to pester him, or the marketing manager, until the book has been in stores for at least a week and some publicity has hit.

Q: What's the key to getting on the *New York Times* bestseller list?
A: I'll assume you mean besides payoffs and prayer. First, there have to be lots of books in lots of stores. Second, there must be visibility—out by the cash register, not back in the military history or psychology sections. If people can't find it, people can't buy it. Third, make the media "pop" in one week—all running and airing at the same time. Fourth, cram the tour—do as many cities and as many events in one single week as a human can do (and make sure the stores where you speak report to the *New York Times* bestseller list; if in doubt, just ask the store—the *New York Times* won't tell you). Fifth, make sure someone on your publisher's staff has told the *New York Times* to track it (and sent their list folks a copy). Otherwise, by the time they catch on to the fact that it's selling and start tracking it, it may no longer be selling well enough to make the list. And keep this fact in mind: if you miss the gold you can still get the silver. The *New York Times* also has an "Extended Bestseller List" (viewable via their Web site).

Q: How can I get my book out of its section in the bookstore and onto the front table, or on one of those fixtures at the end of the aisle?
A: If it can be done, it won't be cheap. For the chains (stores like Borders, B&N, and Walden) publishers have to pay—handsomely—for that kind of "real estate." It's a contract that they have to enter into with the store's national buyer for your specific subject area. And, even if your publisher is willing to pay, the buyer won't offer them the option unless they feel your book would be appropriate for this kind of treatment. Amazon.com has a similar program, but it's for space on their home pages rather than table or "endcap" space. The best thing you can do is speak with your marketing manager about all of this. The good news is, for the independents, front table placement is at each store's discretion—which means it's something you can influence by contacting the store yourself.

Q: What do I do if I'm hearing bookstores aren't carrying my book?
A: Unfortunately, not every bookstore—chain or independent—can carry every book. And those that do carry your book may sell out of them, and may not place a re-order. If you know of people who are looking for your book and can't find a store that stocks it, advise them to purchase online or to ask their store to special order (most stores are quite willing to, and most don't charge a fee). If you can get specific names of stores that aren't carrying your book, and if they're key independents, do let your publisher know. A single call from the local rep may be all it takes to get them to stock it. Also, if you see a pattern within a chain—for example, if people consistently can't locate it at Borders—there may be a distribution glitch, so notify your publisher.

Q: How can I find out which bookstores are stocking my book?
A: There was a time when it was easy for a publisher to know which stores stocked a particular title because the books were

purchased directly from them. Nowadays, many publishers contract with a distributor, which puts a middle man between them
and the stores and makes it harder to tell which books are where.
Furthermore, many bookstores now purchase their books from
wholesalers such as Ingram and Baker & Taylor, in which case specific data is just not available. If the store gets your book from a
wholesaler who gets it from a distributor . . . well, as you can
imagine—it's really hard to tell.

**Q: What if my book is shelved in the wrong section? Can I get
the store to move it?**
A: Independent bookstores shelve books in the section they feel
is most appropriate. Common sections include fiction, poetry,
business, self-help, health, science, art and photography, cooking,
travel, children's, biography, and general nonfiction (which can
include everything from history to current affairs to literary
essays). Many books list the suggested section—or sections—on
the inside flaps (for hardcovers) or on the back of the book (for
paperbacks). That helps your book get to the right place, but it's
no guarantee that it won't go astray. Human error is a factor.
When a bookstore staffer is shelving a book, he frequently just
glances at it and bases the location on the cover art. If he see
a flower on the cover, it goes in the gardening section. If he
sees a baby on the cover, it goes in the parenting section. Nev-
ermind that the book with the flower was actually a collection
of poetry, and the book with the baby was a novel about a
woman who had just given birth. So if you're visiting an indie
and see that your book is in the wrong place, feel free to politely
ask them to move it. You're doing them a favor by helping it
find the right home.

As for the chains, the section that houses your book depends on
the national buyer who purchased the book, and the stores won't be

open to making a change. While this is frustrating, recognize that there may have been method to the madness. For example, we recently published a sports business book. After great debate in-house, we sold it to the sports buyer at one chain and the business buyer at another. The reason? The sports section of the first chain was stronger than its business section (meaning that section tended to move more books in stores) and the business buyer at the second chain tended to make a more aggressive purchase of our books than the sports buyer.

Q: If I'm giving a talk about my book but it isn't in a bookstore, is there a way to arrange for books to be available at the event?
A: For this, there are four options: have a bookstore sell them (known as an "off-site," this is something that they'll only do if you're speaking to at least 50 people; otherwise, they won't think it's worth their time or expense), sell books yourself, have the host organization sell them, or get the host to purchases copies to give to attendees. If you can get the host to go for last option, it means a definite sale. They can purchase the books direct from the publisher (who can usually give a substantial discount) or from their local bookstore (which may also give a discount and which may report to bestseller lists). The publisher's ability to make these things happen is contingent upon your notifying them of your plans well in advance of the event—at minimum, two weeks. Note: for business books, there's another option—800CEOread (http://www.1800ceoread.com). If your host is (or is willing to become) one of 800CEOread's corporate clients, they can purchase your book from them directly. They offer discounts, report to the *New York Times* bestseller list, have their own bestseller list that gets published in various newspapers, and can customize the order by stickering the books with your host's logo, inserting your host's marketing materials, etc. To find out more, go to http://www.1800ceoread.com/volume.asp. A second note: If you're

selling books yourself and the event is out of town, ask to have them shipped to your hotel. There's nothing worse than having to lug a box of books on an airplane.

QUESTIONS FOR OR ABOUT YOUR PUBLICIST

Q: What if I suspect my in-house publicist is lazy?
A: If she really is lazy, you owe it to yourself and your book to speak up. Try talking with her directly. If that doesn't work, ask your editor to have a word with the publicist on your behalf. If that doesn't do the trick, approach your publicist's boss. But keep in mind that authors frequently mistake focus for laziness when the focus is not on their book. If your book is not an in-house priority, your publicist is right to concentrate on other titles that have been deemed by her superiors as having more potential. Remember, ultimately, her loyalty must be to the house, not to you. If you're hearing loud and clear that your book is not a priority for her, consider hiring a freelance publicist.

Q: What if my publicist is young or inexperienced?
A: My honest advice: give her a chance. True, she may not have the contacts or savvy of a more seasoned publicist. But her enthusiasm and energy may well make up for it, and because she doesn't have to attend so many meetings, she'll have more time for follow-up calls to the media on behalf of your book.

Q: Is it okay to ask my publicist to show me the press release before it's sent out?
A: Absolutely! It's your book and you need to make sure it's being represented accurately and well. Just keep in mind that it's the publicist's name that goes at the top of that release, and she needs to feel comfortable with it too—especially since it's going to her contacts. Besides,

she knows the media's likes and dislikes better than you do, and sometimes a publicist can lend a healthy perspective—one that's quite different from your own (very close and not exactly objective) one.

Q: Is it okay to ask my publicist how many galleys/books she's sending out, and what's a normal amount?
A: Yes, it's fine to ask her. For books, two percent of the actual print run (not to be confused with the "announced" first printing, which is a goal number your publisher gives to its sales force— and to the media) is standard. Galley quantities usually range from one hundred to three hundred, depending on the book. The more review-driven your book, the more galleys that need to be sent out. Parenting, health, and business books, for example, are not particularly review-driven. Biographies, memoirs, novels, short-story collections, and poetry are very review-driven.

Q: Is it okay to ask my publicist for a list of media to whom she's sending my book?
A: Yes, of course. I often share these lists with my authors in the hope they'll let me know of anyone whom I might have overlooked. My view is that two heads are better than one when it comes to this stuff. However, I'll warn you that some publicists prefer not to share their lists, and that it is their prerogative not to do so. Sometimes, assuring them that you will keep the list confidential will assuage their concern. A publicist's greatest asset is her contacts, so you can understand why she may be a bit hesitant to share them.

Q: If, after my book comes out, my travels take me to a good media town, does it make sense to ask my publicist to see what she can book?
A: You bet, provided it's a recent pub (three months old, max). Just be sure to give your publicist a fair amount of notice; some shows

fill their calendars with guests months in advance, especially those that air weekends or only once a week. If your publicist is unwilling or unable to do this outreach, you can always do it yourself. Or, if you're traveling to speak at a school, for a company, or for a group, ask your host if they have plans to reach out to the press. If they don't, encourage them. If they do, forward along your press material as well as recent clips. It might even be worth sending them a few books to use in their efforts. Your publicist should be willing to do this; if not, it's worth doing yourself.

Q: My publicist says my new book has great "backlist" potential. So why isn't she putting forth more effort on its behalf?

A: Editors buy books for two main reasons—because they have good frontlist potential or good backlist potential (on rare occasions, a book has both). The former are a "flash in the pan." They have a short but hopefully glorious sales life. 2003's *I Am the Central Park Jogger* is one example, as is pretty much any book of fiction. Frontlist books are publicity-dependent. They need to go out strong with the media. Backlist books are those that "have legs." They're often reference books like this one—or health or investment guides. They won't make it onto bestseller lists, but over years they could outsell a one-week bestseller ten to one. They're the tortoise, not the hare. They're the one you marry, not the one you date. Starting to get the picture? Your publicist, knowing this is how things are, relaxes. She cannot make or break your book. It will be fine without her. It will, through the magic of time—and more than a little word-of-mouth—find its core audience and be embraced by them. Sure, there are things she can do to help it along—coverage in relevant journals, perhaps. But your book won't tank if she doesn't get *Oprah.* My advice: stay on her. And in the meantime, think "grassroots" and get out there and hustle.

MISCELLANEOUS QUESTIONS

Q: How can I get more copies of my book?

A: By contract, each author receives a certain number of complimentary copies (usually twenty or so). If you anticipate needing a lot of them to support your own promotional efforts, try to get it written into your contract. If it's too late for that, your publicist should be willing to send you some extra copies if you give her specifics on what you plan to do with them (e.g., target radio in your home town, do a mailing to special-interest publications). If your plans for the books fall into the category of marketing, course adoption, or special sales (meaning sales to cataloguers like Bas Bleu or Land's End, corporations, specialty stores like gift shops or hardware stores, etc.), you're better off asking the people in charge of those duties at your publisher to ship you books directly. Many houses monitor the number of copies publicists go through, and you want to save her copies for media use alone. If all else fails, your publicist should be able to give you a customer service number that you can use to order books. Note: by contract, most authors are entitled to a substantial (e.g., forty or fifty percent) discount on their own title, so be sure to let the customer service rep know that you're the author of the book you're ordering.

Q: What if I know of a professor who might assign my book?

A: It's great for authors to push for their books to be course adopted. Course adoptions are a renewable resource. Once professors teach your book, they're likely to do it again and again—if for no other reason than they don't want to have to come up with a new lesson plan. That means each new semester could lead to the sale of hundreds of copies of your book. So ask your publicist for the name of the person who handles academic marketing, and shoot him an e-mail with your contacts and ideas. If he's not responsive, by all means send the prof a book yourself. Keep in mind that hardcovers are rarely course adopted; most professors don't put a book on the syllabus until it's out in paperback so as to keep costs down for students.

Q: Should I throw a launch party for my book?
A: There are really three kinds of launch parties. The first is the big New York City kind, where a room is rented out, formal invitations are printed, gift bags (which include a free copy of the book as well as other goodies) are stuffed, and a guest list is labored over so that no VIP or media titan is missed. As an example, when I was at Houghton Mifflin, we published David Halberstam's *Best American Sports Writing of the Century*, and the party—co-hosted by *Vanity Fair*— was held at the New York City landmark restaurant Elaine's. Guests included such notables as Charlie Rose, Tom Brokaw, and Chip McGrath (editor of the *New York Times Book Review*). These kinds of parties are usually paid for by the publisher, and believe me they're super expensive. That means they cannot be done for every book. Your publisher will throw this kind of party for you if yours is a lead title *and* if you're a celebrity who can draw a crowd (and not just *any* crowd—the kind of people whose mere attendance increases the publisher's clout) or if the publication of your book marks some kind of landmark (such as the culmination of the publisher's efforts to establish a new imprint or launch a new series).

The second kind of launch party takes place in your living room. It includes family and friends and favorite foods, and a toast to you by someone you love.

Both of these types of events have value. The first creates buzz for your book (you've gotta love those gossip-column write-ups). The second gives you the opportunity to share your accomplishment with those who matter most, and to fortify you against any bad reviews your book may receive. The third kind of party is the useless kind. It's held in your employer's conference room. It draws second-tier media (and only a few), and feels rather awkward for all who attend. Cheap food (and not enough), cheap wine (for some, too much), and a pile of books in the corner for sale (by the end of the night, you've sold two). Who needs it!

If you or your employer decide to throw a launch party, do not ask your publisher to chip in financially. Aside from the fact that they won't appreciate your hitting them up for the cash, it's not something for which they will have budgeted, and any money they do allot out of guilt or embarrassment would have to be taken from somewhere else (such as your book's ad campaign). Instead, simply invite key members of your publishing team (your publicist, your book's marketing manager, the sales director, the publisher, etc.) to the party. Perhaps they'll go the classy route and send over a case of champagne or some flowers to use as a centerpiece.

Q: Do I need a Web site for my book?
A: It couldn't hurt—especially if you plan to do a Web campaign for your book. A good author Web site includes the following: a description of the book, a shot of the book cover, your photo, your bio, an excerpt from the book, blurbs for the book, and quotes from reviews of the book. It should link to an online bookseller— or several so that guests have a choice—and should have your e-mail address so that fans of your book can make contact. A list of talks you're giving and your radio and TV appearances would also be helpful. That way, your fans know when they can check you out in person or tune you in.

Q: Will my book be automatically entered for relevant award competitions?
A: Some publishing houses are very good about entering their books for award competitions. Others completely miss the boat. Talk to your publicist to see if it's something she will handle.

Realize it's not just a commitment of her time (completing the forms can take a while), but also of her budget (many competitions have hefty fees). Keep in mind that, in addition to the major competitions—the National Book Award, the Pulitzer Prize, the *Los Angeles Times* Book Prizes, the National Book Critics Circle Award, the various PEN awards, and, for poetry, the awards of the Academy of American Poets—there are a ton of smaller ones. You should expect your publicist to be familiar with the big ones, but it's your responsibility to alert her to the small fry. Help her out by requesting the entry forms for these second-tier contests, and forwarding them to her. Not sure it's worth your time? Granted, winning the Wisconsin Library Association's annual award for a book written by a Wisconsin author may not skyrocket you onto the bestseller lists. But it could result in a profile piece in the *Milwaukee Journal Sentinel*, which could get you an interview with Wisconsin Public Radio's nationally syndicated *To the Best of Our Knowledge*. Starting to sound a little more worth the effort, isn't it?

Q: Is there a local organization to which I can turn for support when my book is published?
A: Since 1984, all fifty states and the District of Columbia have had a statewide center for the book. Each is affiliated with the Library of Congress's Center for the Book. According to the Library's Web site, each center's goal is to "promote their own state's book culture and literary heritage." Many of them sponsor literary festivals or have an author reading series. Some publish newsletters that mention books by local authors or note books of local interest. Reach out to yours to see what resources and opportunities are available. Contact info for each state center can be found at http://www.loc.gov/loc/cfbook/stacen.html. Many states also have a Council for the Humanities that sponsors literary events, offers grants and awards, and supports authors in other important ways.

Chapter 8

The Art of the Interview

For years, I've listened to my authors on the radio, watched them on TV, and read profile pieces about them and feature articles in which they're quoted. I've learned a lot from them. I've also learned a lot from the various reporters, editors, and producers who've gone through me to gain access to these scribes. Sometimes, after an interview, they'll call me to say thanks and tell me what a great job the author has just done. A few have sent thank-you gifts for me to forward on. Other times, when things go wrong, they'll call me so I know that a first-time author had a panic attack—on camera, no less—or a seasoned one was brilliant but arrived an hour late. I've gotten calls about narcoleptic novelists (note to self: don't book him before noon), bitchy biographers ("Did you even *read* my book?"), and positively puzzled poets ("Which book of mine are we speaking of again?"). There are common themes, to be sure. And they lend themselves to some general pointers.

GENERAL TIPS

Whether it's print or broadcast, night or day, live or taped, big circ or local rag, never, and I mean *never*, express disdain to interviewers whom you suspect hasn't read your book. It is, quite frankly, not their job to ponder every or *any* word you've written. Their job is simply to fill the page or the air, in an interesting way, with interesting people. While many hosts and reporters pride themselves in reading some if not all of each book they discuss, it's the exception, not the norm. In the words of Anneli Rufus, Books Editor of San Francisco's *East Bay Express* and herself author of *Party of One*, "Assume the worst-case scenario, which is that the interviewer will know absolutely nothing about the book, will not have read a single word of it. That is unfortunately the case far too often, so realize this in advance and don't take it personally." Remember, you need this person more than they need you. It doesn't pay to piss them off. And while you're at it, don't take it for granted that the audience—the viewer of TV, the listener of radio, the reader of newspapers and magazines—has cracked the spine. In the words of Annette Heist—who does approximately two forty-minute author interviews a month as producer at National Public Radio's *Talk of the Nation Science Friday*—"Don't assume that everyone has read your book. I think it is safer to assume that no one has read it."

Never underestimate the importance of soundbites. A soundbite is a turn of phrase, a quip, a clever statement said with authority. It's controversial, or brilliant, or funny, or profound. You know you're soundbiting well when what you say is called out in a "pull quote" (those sentences that newspaper and magazine reporters repeat in larger font elsewhere in the article) or used as a "tease" for a radio or TV segment (a tease is a quote used to promo a segment). If you're one of several people being interviewed, a good soundbite makes it impossible for a reporter or producer not to include you in their piece. The best way to become soundbite proficient is to imagine ahead of time the kinds of questions you'll be asked, and practice your answers to them. That way, when someone says, "Why did you write this book?," your response will be, "Because I saw a glaring need for this kind of information" rather than, "Well, I guess I hoped it might be helpful to someone."

That said, guard against practicing too much. According to Rufus, "A good interview is one in which the author says something that he or she has *not* said to anyone else." Dennis Lythgoe, who in his role as Books Editor at Utah's *Deseret News* does about six author interviews a month, says, "I would rather have a natural, off-the-cuff feel to the interview, rather than talk to an author who has a set of notes to go by."

So what else makes an interview good? Rufus says, "It is helpful when an author can recount an anecdote. For instance, an interviewer might ask, 'What was the most surprising thing you learned while working on this book?' or 'How did you get the scenes set in Jamaica to feel so authentic?' Anecdotes are like gold in a print or broadcast interview—unless they go on for too long." Lythgoe looks for "an author who is friendly, kind and willing to talk. My *very* favorite is the occasional author who will actually ask *me* two or three questions (naturally curious type) . . . I like to feel that the author is actually enjoying the process." He also says, "I'd love it if the author was candid, witty, and forthcoming about the nature of the book, how it was conceived and the problems they had writing it. This stuff is interesting to the reader."

Robin Dougherty—who interviews two or three authors a month and has a regular column called "Between the Lines" in the *Boston Sunday Globe*'s "Books" section—says, "A good author interview is one in which I made some kind of unique connection with the author that I can pass on to my readers . . . I like to be surprised a little and to find out something I didn't know—about them or their subject. Something that sheds light on their creative process or perhaps says something about the state of literature. I also like quirky stories—not that they should come prepared with them, but if a question elicits an entertaining answer, I'm always thrilled."

Armin Brott, author of *The Expectant Father* and host of *Positive Parenting*—which airs on San Francisco's KOIT Radio and includes one or two thirty-minute author interviews most weeks—says a good interview is "one where I feel that the audience goes away with the feeling of having eavesdropped on a really interesting conversation, one where I as the host have learned something, too. One way I can usually tell is by looking at the clock: if time is really flying, I know the interview is a good one. If every second seems to drag, I know it's a problem."

Speaking of problems, what do authors do that's *not* helpful during interviews? Lythgoe says, "I ask questions that I hope will elicit more than a one-word or one-sentence response—there are still some authors who are too tight-lipped." NPR's Heist echoes with, "The only problems that come to mind are when authors give answers that are too short, answering simply 'yes' or 'no' to questions." According to Lythgoe, it's also important never to cut the interview itself short: "I prefer the author be relaxed and not say 'I have a dental appointment in fifteen minutes so let's get this over with fast!' or 'I think you've got enough, don't you?'"

Dougherty's pet peeve: "Giving me the same quotes they are giving anyone else. I try to ask questions in a way that prevents this from happening, and I also know they probably aren't aware of how often they are repeating the same banter, but it's infuriating to find the same quotes in another interview."

So what can you do to prepare for an interview? For starters, plan your day so that there's no danger of your missing it. Dougherty says, "I don't think there's anything an author needs to do to prepare, other than to show up for the interview. This is a bigger problem with actors than with writers usually, but I've had a few mishaps. One writer scheduled a 10:00 A.M. interview with me, then took her cell phone with her as she went out all day on a fishing boat. At some point she realized she was out of range, but there was no way for her to contact me and I sat by the phone, fuming, on deadline, as I waited for her call. Needless to say I wasn't in a great frame of mind for the interview when she came back to port and then called me from a land line around 5:00 P.M."

Dougherty also stresses the importance of being ready for difficult questions. She says "Authors should be prepared for a question that makes them uncomfortable. If their last book was a bomb, and they are a household name, I am probably going to bring it up. My object is not to put the author on edge—it's to serve the legitimate concerns and curiosity of my readers. I certainly am not going to ask personal information that's not pertinent, but, say, if your last book was a much-ridiculed biography of Ronald Reagan narrated by a fictional character in first person, and your next book is written in a completely different narrative style, I am probably going to ask you to talk about it."

Besides steeling yourself for the Spanish Inquisition, what else can you do to prep? NPR's Heist says, "An author might find it helpful to listen to the show. The show doesn't air everywhere, but archived versions are available on the Web. This might help an author feel more comfortable with the format of the show, and to get a feel for the types of questions that might be asked."

KOIT's Brott also suggests you do some research prior to going on air. He says, "Find out a little about the interview. As a minimum, how long is it? Who's the interviewer? What are the audience demographics? What's the format? Do you think the host will be sympathetic or antagonistic." He also points out that "preparing for a five-minute interview is a very different thing than a thirty-minute one. Know the main points you want to make and tailor them to the specific show. A five-minute show means probably one point, a longer show you may be able to get more in."

It's a good idea to at least thumb through your book prior to your interview. As Devorah Lissek—who in her role as producer at WHYY's *Radio Times* (NPR, Philly) does three to five one-hour-long author interviews a week—explains, "By the time the book tour comes along many times the author's head is already in a different place, working on the next book or project. So refresh your memory."

Radio and TV producers will sometimes provide you with the

questions they're going to ask beforehand (especially if the inter-view will be live), but most prefer not to because they want your responses to seem fresh rather than rehearsed. If you're asked a question to which you don't know the answer, try not to say, "I have no idea" or "that's outside my area of expertise." Says Rufus, "It isn't helpful when an interviewee just says, 'I don't know. I never thought of that.' " An interviewee should try to answer every question. If that's impossible, he or she should be prepared to say, "I don't know, but it reminds me of something else that's relevant, and that is . . ." Above all else, never lie—the host could call you on it then and there, or it could come back to haunt you later.

Newspaper and magazine reporters almost never provide their questions ahead of time, though these days some reporters conduct their interviews by e-mail. This is actually a nice way to go about things because it gives you time to craft a great response. It also guar-antees you won't be misquoted and keeps your quotes from being taken out of context. Remember, most journalists don't share their articles—or the quotes they're using—with the people they've interviewed prior to publication. When asked whether she observes this practice, the *Globe*'s Dougherty said, "Absolutely not . . . I'm not writing P.R. for them. I'm writing something that serves my readers. I've been asked this in other parts of my career as a journalist and I'll happily read back quotes to someone if they are nervous about not sounding articulate. I will also make a follow-up call to the author or publicist for fact-checking if I find that my notes are missing something crucial, but I'm not trying to please the author. There is no need for them to sign off on my column."

To sum it up, whether you're doing a print or broadcast inter-view, your goal should be two-fold: to give an interview that sells books and to give an interview that makes the host or reporter want to speak with you again (either to talk about your next book or to comment on current events—remember, this person's

Rolodex is one you want to be on). So give it your full attention. Be punctual and polite. Be sure not to slip into industry jargon on general-interest shows. And for goodness sake, don't forget to write down the name of the person with whom you spoke. In fact, if possible, send him a thank-you e-mail once the segment airs or the article is published, letting him know that you liked the piece and are at his disposal if he needs you in the future. In the words of Heist, the best way to get back on a show is to "be nice to the producer." Of course, as WHYY's Lissek points out, it doesn't hurt to "have something else to talk about for an hour."

TIPS FOR PRINT INTERVIEWS

The cardinal rule for interviews with newspaper and magazine reporters is *don't say it if you don't want it to be printed*—not even "off-the-record." Also, no matter what, keep your answers somewhat succinct. If you blather on, the reporter will quote somebody else simply because it's easier.

If reporters call you directly and say they're on deadline, do the interview then and there—don't ask them if you can do it later or tell them to call your publicist to arrange another time. However, do get their e-mail address, phone number, and physical address. Pass that info to your publicist right away so that she can messenger or overnight your book—or at least e-mail your press material. This way, they're more likely to identify you as "author of" in the piece.

If you have prep time for the interview, use it to its fullest. Hit the Web and find out what you can about the interviewer. Read some of his articles by going to his publication's Web site and typing his name in the search box. Google him if you have to (and you'll have to if he's freelance). Note: this kind of prep work can also be done for radio and TV, usually just by hitting the show's site. Click on the section marked "meet our team," or "about us," or whatever they call it, and read up on the person who'll be interviewing you.

As editor-at-large of *Pages*, a bimonthly magazine for booklovers (http://www.ireadpages.com) Bethanne Kelly Patrick does two to four major author interviews a month, plus a few minor ones by e-mail. Her advice to authors: stay calm. "The more uptight/nervous/anxious/uncomfortable an author is, the worse the interview is going to be. At first this might seem to be more of a handicap for the journalist/interviewer—but remember, even if you give the most sanitized of soundbites, your attitude and demeanor are going to come across in the finished piece if said journalist does his job right."

What should you do at the start of your newspaper or magazine interview? Patrick says, "State upfront how much time is available, and if there are any likely distractions (pet prone to making noise, family/guests in vicinity, bad connection, etc.)." How many questions should you expect to have to field during the course of the interview? According to Patrick, "fifteen to twenty questions is an hour interview."

Authors often make the mistake of thinking a print interview is over after the reporter's questions stop. This is actually when you need to kick into gear and "close the deal," so to speak. Final impressions count, and this is your chance to land yourself squarely on the reporter's Rolodex for future pieces. Patrick's thoughts on how to do this: "Offer to consider follow-up questions and check specific quotes, especially those that might be complex and/or filled with facts that need to be verified. Ask where and how to get a copy of the interviewer's publication, and offer to share that information with other authors. Provide feedback to your publicist, especially if the interview went well. Offer to sign a copy of the book for the interviewer." Patrick also reminds authors to "remain humble—after all, your interviewer . . . knows lots of other writers, publicists, editors, and journalists—be nice."

TIPS FOR RADIO INTERVIEWS

There are three different ways of doing radio interviews—by phone (commonly referred to as a "phoner"), in-studio, and in-studio via ISDN line.

Phoners are by far the easiest for authors. You can do them from home, from your office, or basically anywhere there's a land line in a quiet place. If you're doing a phoner, it's best not to use a cordless phone because they can create static. If you do have to use a cordless, at least be sure not to pace around. Find a place where the reception is good, and settle down and stay put. Keep in mind that it's never okay to use a cell phone for a phoner. The last thing you want is for the signal to be lost mid-sentence, especially if the interview is *live* (meaning it's being broadcast while it's happening; some interviews are *taped* to be aired at a later date). If you're doing a phoner, the host's producer will usually initiate the call, but it's a good idea for you to have the producer's name and number and the studio number handy just in case. It's also a good idea to have your publicist give them your cell phone number as a backup. If you're ever in a situation where you're supposed to be doing an interview and the station hasn't called, don't hesitate to call their studio line. It's possible they lost your number or copied it down wrong. That said, don't panic if it gets to be five past the hour and the station hasn't called—many shows do news at the top of the hour before they go to their guest.

In-studio interviews are ones that are done at the radio station that's having you on as a guest. While they're less convenient because they require you to schlep there, the sound quality is much better and there's something nice about being able to look your interviewer in the eye. If the interview is live, be sure to arrive ten to fifteen minutes before you're due on air so that you can get set up (they'll need to get a read on your voice and adjust their equipment accordingly, and you'll need time to get used to their mike). If the interview is taped, five minutes will suffice.

When a radio station in another city wants to do an interview with you but needs the sound quality to be better than it would if you did it as a phoner, they'll ask you to go to a local studio and will patch you in to theirs via ISDN line (not to be confused with an ISBN, which is given by the Library of Congress and serves as a sort of social security number for your book). As with a regular in-studio interview, be sure to arrive with plenty of time to spare. Bring with you not only the contact number for the host's producer and their studio, but also the number for the person who will be your contact on-site. This interview will feel much like a phoner, but without the comforts of home.

If bringing a list of all these phone numbers sounds excessive, trust me—it's not. I once had an author who was scheduled for a live, half-hour, in-studio interview on a local Boston station. He arrived there nice and early, only to find that the front door was locked (it was an evening show and, apparently, the intern who normally mans the door was out sick that night). He tried the buzzer—no response. He waited and tried again. He used his cell phone to call the producer, but all he got was voice mail. Unfortunately, he had neglected to bring the studio number with him, and he didn't have my number on him either (hint: keep your publicist's card in your wallet, and make sure it includes her home and cell numbers). Eventually, he gave up and got back in his car. Imagine his chagrin as, driving home with the radio on, he listened to the host say over and over, "I'm sure our guest will be joining us soon."

Authors often ask me how they can make sure their book gets mentioned without having to be the one to plug it (which is, for the record, a super-tacky thing to do). It's usually an irrational fear. Most radio hosts automatically identify their guests as "author of" as a service to their listeners and a courtesy to the guest. They'll usually do so at the start of the interview, leading into or coming back from commercial breaks, and/or at the interview's close. Sometimes, they'll even plug your book in promos that air the day before—or even the morning of—the show, and on their Web site. All of this alleviates the need for you to start every sentence with, "As I say in my book . . ." As KOIT's Brott points out, too many mentions of the book, "especially when they're forced into the conversation by the author, makes the show seem like an infomercial and turns people off. Listeners/viewers want to learn something, not be pitched to."

If you're giving a local talk or reading and want the show to plug the event, it's best to remind the host or producer of this prior to the interview's start. Be prepared to supply them with the details—date, time, and address. That way, you won't have to be the one to say it. Keep in mind that, if the show is produced locally but aired nationally, they probably won't be willing to mention the event since the info won't be relevant to many of their listeners.

If you want to get a little extra airtime for your book, offer to donate a few copies for them to give out to listeners. Though not all shows like to do this, others are pleased to offer your book to the first three callers. They may even make it more fun, awarding your book to the first caller who can tell them the middle name of the person whose biography you've written; the first caller who can name the protagonist in your previous book; the first caller who can guess the number one excuse men give for cheating on their wives in your book about divorce. If you have an idea for such a contest, feel free to suggest it to the producer ahead of time, or ask your publicist to do so.

If your interview is live, keep in mind that callers might get to ask you questions. So that such calls don't take you by surprise, inquire ahead if that will be the format. If so, as WHYY's Lissek suggests, "Refer to callers by name." Keep pen and paper handy so that you can jot them down. You may also have cause to make notes to yourself during the interview, so even if the host won't be taking any calls, have a notebook handy just in case.

Don't be surprised if the radio show's producer asks to speak with you by phone before committing to an interview. NPR's Heist says, "Be willing to talk to the producer, even if you feel that the answers to her questions are covered in your book." It's their way of checking you out—of making sure you can talk about the subject they want to discuss, and that you can do so intelligently. Heist says it's how they "get a feel for how you will answer questions during the 'real' interview." For panel shows, it gives them a chance to make sure your view is different enough from that of their other guest(s). And it's an opportunity for them to make sure your voice is suitable for radio. I once had a wonderful author whose vocal chords were slightly paralyzed. It made his voice sound strained, and he missed out on some radio opportunities because of it. Same with a couple of great authors who had heavy foreign accents. But by and large, most of these discussions with producers lead to actual bookings. FYI, some producers refer to these conversations as "pre-interviews." However, other producers seem to reserve that term for conversations that are held prior to radio and TV interviews that have already been secured—conversations that are used just to go over what will be discussed on-air.

If ever an interview doesn't happen (for whatever reason) and it's one that your publicist booked, be sure to let her know there was a problem so that she can reschedule. If it was the station's fault and they didn't have a good reason (like a change in plans due to breaking news), she can call and bawl them out for wasting your time—and hers. And she'll know not to book with them again. If it was your fault—for example, if you forgot—she can call the station to make amends. This is important for you and for her. You may want to do the show in the future and she has a reputation to maintain. Just a few weeks prior to writing these pages, I received an angry call from a drive-time host in New Orleans. He proceeded to inform me that the interview I'd arranged a month ago had never taken place and that his efforts to reschedule with the author directly had largely been ignored. I was shocked! Neither he nor the author had notified me when things went sour. To my knowledge the interview had happened and gone well. I was, in the end, able to reschedule, but I'll be slow to book that show again. As for the author, if he doesn't protect the fruits of my labor (the bookings), I can't be expected to protect the fruits of his (the book).

When doing a radio interview, a few simple rules apply. For starters, take a deep breath. According to Jeff Schechtman, host and producer at KVON, the ABC radio affiliate in Napa, California, who interviews at least ten or fifteen authors each week, "By the time the author is conducting interviews he or she usually knows the subject matter thoroughly. The most important thing is to relax. This is not a lecture or a quiz. It is telling a story about the work and engaging in a conversation about the subject." If you're really feeling nervous, or just need a warm-up exercise, you might want to chat with a spouse or friend about the book in the minutes leading up to your interview, just to start the flow. Second, don't talk over the host, the other guests if there are some (you won't always be the only person invited on to talk about an issue), or the listeners if the show is taking callers. Also, don't interrupt. As WHYY's Lissek says, "Understand the give and take of an interview." Third, don't be hostile. Keep your cool no matter how dimwitted or insensitive the question. If a host, or fellow guest, or caller seems hell-bent on getting your goat, don't rise to the occasion. Always take the high road. He or she will look like nothing but a jerk so long as you stay calm. Fourth, watch your mouth. The show could get fined if you let a swear slip out. Fifth, don't ramble. Most of your answers should hover around the fifteen-second mark. And sixth, master the art of answering the question that should have been asked instead of the question that was asked. If someone says, "Do you think historians will like your book?" and your book is meant to appeal to a more general audience, respond with, "I do, though it was written with the layperson in mind. I think it will appeal to the general reader because . . ." If you're asked a rather obvious question, or a rather stupid one, do the same thing—answer it quickly and then move on to what you want to discuss. Most of these rules hold true for TV, too.

TIPS FOR TV INTERVIEWS

Just like there are three different ways of doing radio interviews, there are three different ways of doing TV interviews—in the studio of the station that's broadcasting the interview, in a local studio with an ISDN line hook-up to the studio from which the show originates, or at a location other than a studio with a mobile camera crew. Regardless of the method, the interview can be live or taped.

If your interview is done in-studio, you may have to spend some time in the greenroom. Think of it as a bullpen for television guests. Someone will escort you to it, and someone will escort you from it and into the studio at interview time—and back again when you're done. Some greenrooms are chock full of goodies, and most of these tantalizing items should be avoided. Soda can make you burp. Fruit juices can stain your clothes. Cheese can cause you to have to clear your throat. Other food can get caught in your teeth. If you're thirsty, drink water. If you're so hungry you think you'll pass out or fear your stomach will rumble audibly during your interview, have crackers or a muffin—in other words, something safe.

For in-studio interviews, wear solid colors, dark or bright. Patterns tend to be distracting and white works poorly for TV. Men should wear a tie and jacket or sport coat. Women should wear a suit or a nice sweater-set. Don't wear anything distracting in your hair like a headband, clip, or scrunchy. Women should wear makeup—base to even out your skin tone, mascara to make your eyes stand out, and lipstick and blush so as not to look washed out. There will usually be someone there to do your makeup for you if you ask, but don't count on it. Men will probably be given the option of wearing a little makeup. I would advise at least some lip color, and powder if you're shiny. Both are easy enough to wipe off after. During your interview, don't fidget or touch your face. Avoid a lot of gestures or talking with your hands. Don't take a sip of water unless your mouth goes dry (it's distracting to your viewers, and you could choke or spill). Be conscious of your posture, and men, take a second to smooth your tie and coat.

If your interview is done away from a studio and if it's taped, it's conceivable that a TV crew will tell you that they need to get B-roll. B-roll is miscellaneous footage that is woven throughout a segment to round it out. It may be you walking down the street, eating in your favorite restaurant, typing at your computer, or autographing your book. It will be used as filler for the narrated parts of your segment. In other words, it will serve as backdrop for the narrator's voice. There's nothing like B-roll to make you feel self-conscious. In fact, sometimes it can feel plain silly. Try to grin and bear it, but if you're asked to do something that feels really hokey or out of character, you're within your rights to put your foot down. For an author's take on B-roll, check out Jonathan Franzen's "Meet Me in St. Louis," an essay about his *Oprah* experience that can be found in his book *How to Be Alone* (Farrar, Straus and Giroux, 2002).

Authors often ask how they can get tape of their radio or TV appearance. The key is to not be shy about asking since the producer probably won't offer. However, you must think ahead. Producers don't like to receive this kind of request after the fact—and truth be told, neither do publicists. If you want a tape—and it's a great idea to get one, particularly if it's TV—and cannot tape the appearance yourself or have someone tape it for you, the best thing to do is ask the show for a tape at the time of the interview. If it's an in-studio interview and you show up with a blank VHS (for TV) or audio (for radio) tape, they'll be more likely to do it for you, as it won't cost them anything. If all else fails, for radio shows, you might be able to access the interview online using Real Audio, and for TV shows, you can order a tape from a company called Video Monitoring Service. VMS isn't cheap (over a hundred bucks), but often times it's worth it. The quality is better, and they'll splice the tease and the interview together so that it's almost seamless (in other words, they'll remove the commercial). If you're on multiple segments, they'll remove the commercials throughout. One last suggestion—if tape is hard to come by, ask the producer whether they provide transcripts. Some shows do—some even post them on their sites.

TIPS FOR WEB SITE CHATS

Web site chats are less popular than they once were, but they can still be a decent medium for promoting your book—especially on sites like WebMD.com, which archive their transcripts. All Web site chats are live, and all have a host or moderator who will keep the conversation moving and plug your book for you. There are two different ways to do these chats—by logging on from your own computer using a password, or by doing the chat over the telephone with a "translator" or "scribe." This is a person who reads the questions participants are posing, relays them to you verbally, and types in your responses as you speak them so that participants get the answers they desire. Sometimes, the moderator doubles as the scribe.

When doing a Web site chat, be careful when giving out advice—particularly medical advice. Make sure there is an appropriate disclaimer, such as, "This chat is not meant to take the place of a visit with your physician."

If you want to be actively involved in the Web promotion of your book but a live chat doesn't fit your schedule, consider moderating a message board like the ones on Parents.com, the Web site of *Parents* magazine. They're a great way to further establish yourself as an expert and communicate with potential readers directly. They're also a nice way to keep your finger on the pulse of America. If you moderate a message board on a fitness site, for example, it won't be long before you learn what questions people are really asking about exercise and nutrition.

Message boards work like this: participants post questions and you log on and answer them at your convenience using a special access code. Message boards can last any length of time, but usually go for a week or a month. When it comes to message boards try to answer as many questions as possible, even if it means not answering any one question as thoroughly as you'd like. The key is to keep folks from feeling ignored. It's completely appropriate to refer participants to relevant sections of your book for further information.

Chapter 9

Creating "Buzz"

I'll let you in on every publicist's dirty little secret: media alone cannot a bestseller make. We publicists take a certain martyristic pleasure in thinking that every book lives and dies in our lap. And while I wouldn't sneeze at the chance for a *New York Times* book review, or a stint on NPR, or a morning show booking, the truth is that none of them—or even all of them together—will necessarily skyrocket a book to success. Publicity is merely a means to an end . . . and that end is something called "buzz."

"Buzz," a.k.a. "word-of-mouth," is the beautiful thing that occurs when your book takes on a life of its own. We know buzz is happening when the media starts calling—media to which we haven't sent your book. There are other things that alert us, too—calls from reading groups, calls from organizations that want you to speak, even calls from readers who want to get in touch with you. In short, it's when people seek us out instead of us having to seek them out. It's an indication that your book is being talked about even though we didn't start the conversation.

But buzz is, of course, elusive. We're not *sure* how to make it. If we knew, let's face it—there'd be lots more bestsellers. That said, there are things that can be done on a grassroots level to get people talking—to get the chain reaction going.

There seems to be two main ways to create buzz for a book. One is to reach out directly to potential readers. The other is to reach out to booksellers in the hope that they'll "hand-sell"—a term we use to describe it when they recommend your book to their customers.

REACHING OUT TO READERS

Web Campaigns

If your publicist isn't already doing Web outreach, you can use e-mail to obtain mentions in e-newsletters and on subject-specific websites (for example, if your book is about animal rights, approach the person in charge of content for the Humane Society's site). Offer them brief excerpts or a "canned" interview (your Q&A), as well as cover art and your photo. You can even suggest someone on their staff interview you for an original piece.

Also, send your book to people who have good Weblogs (a.k.a. "blogs")—personal sites used to express one person's views on a wide range of topics (they differ from a regular Web site in that the person posts new content each day in a diary-like format, with lots of links to articles and other blogs of interest). If the bloggers like your book, rest assured they'll write about it. There are tons of good blogs out there, but some of the best ones are those of journalists. For a list, go to http://www.cyberjournalist.net. A section called J-Blogs (for journalists' weblogs) will have the necessary links. To monitor your book's mentions on blogs, go to http://allconsuming.net or http://www.onfocus.com/bookwatch.

Remember, if you or your publicist don't have time to do a Web campaign for your book, there are people who can be paid to do it for you.

Mailing Lists

Some publishers are willing to purchase mailing lists from organizations that are appropriate for a particular book. They then create brochures to disseminate. For example, a couple of years ago we bought a list of the country's top personal trainers and mailed them information about our book *Hot Point Fitness*. You can help your publisher by researching organizations that might have such lists to sell. Some organizations even provide these lists free to members, in which case you might want to consider joining.

"Big-Mouth" Mailings

Either your editor or your book's marketing manager should be willing to do a "big-mouth" mailing for you. This is simply a mailing to key people who may be inclined and able to spread the word about your book—people with a platform who can talk it up. They should be VIP writers or VIPs in whatever field your book is about. For example, if it's a novel set in New England, you may want to have it sent to John Updike, Anita Shreve, and Chris Bohjalian. A book about the ocean could go to Linda Greenlaw and Sebastian Junger. If it's a book on the fight against cancer, consider having it sent to the director of the American Cancer Society and to some celebrities who publicly support the cause. A collection of poetry might go to David Lehman (who edits the *Best American Poetry* series), the current poet laureate of the country and your state, and the directors of the Poetry Society of America and the American Academy of Poets. If it's a book on management, it makes sense to have it sent to influential CEOs and other heads of corporations—especially ones with whom you have a personal connection.

The books should be sent with a note (one clearly addressed to the person to whom it's going—not a "Dear Friend" form letter). It can be written by you—even *handwritten* by you on elegant stationery. Or it can be on company letterhead, written by your editor or marketing manager. Regardless of who is writing the letter, the mailing should go out from the publisher (in other words, you shouldn't have to eat the postage costs). So if you're doing the writing, send along the notes once they're done, and provide labels, if possible. If not, at least provide complete addresses (the editor or marketing manager shouldn't have to do the research).

How many books are we talking about? Twenty to twenty-five is a reasonable amount to expect. If you want to send out more than that, you can always ask, and if your request is denied you can buy copies at your author's discount and send them out yourself.

By the way, use finished books for this, not galleys. Galleys are less impressive and more expensive, plus you want to reserve this kind of buzz until books have hit stores.

Flyers

It's a good idea to create a flyer for your book—one that can be sent to conferences for their literature tables. Your marketing manager should be willing to design such a flyer for this purpose. If not, you can do it yourself quite easily. Just steal a few descriptive paragraphs from your press release, throw in a few quotes from reviews, drop in cover art (you can get a jpeg or tif file from your publicist), and add ordering information (your marketing manager can provide you with the correct language and contact info, preferably a toll-free number; if all else fails, just say "available wherever books are sold"). You might also want to include a brief bio (just a sentence or two) and your photo—but only if it looks professional. Here's an example of a flyer created for this book.

**The Savvy Author's Guide
to Book Publicity**
*A Comprehensive Resource—
From Building the Buzz to Pitching the Press*
LISSA WARREN

**From a leading publicity director in the book industry—
an essential guide for authors to getting maximum exposure
for any kind of book**

Here is an essential reference for writers—from the self-published to those published by major hous-es—written by a leading book publicist who pitches books to media every day of her working life. Tapping into her years publicizing such authors as pediatrician Dr. T. Berry Brazelton, poet Mary Oliver, and economist John Kenneth Galbraith, Da Capo Press Senior Director of Publicity Lissa Warren covers book promotion *with* a publicist, *without* a publicist, and when a publicist isn't getting results. Each chapter details what happens to a book once it's off press, and how authors can be help-ful in the promotion process—or even spearhead it if necessary—to get the coverage they deserve.

Warren's advice is buttressed by her stories of authors—the enterprising, the shy, the veteran, and the novice—relating tours gone awry, bestsellers made and almost made, and great and not-so-great author/publicist collaboration. *The Savvy Author's Guide to Book Publicity* covers every-thing from how to develop press material and target the right shows and publications, to follow-ing up effectively with the media and hiring people who can help ensure that every bookseller and consumer has a chance to hear an author's message loud and clear.

Lissa Warren has worked in the publicity departments of David R. Godine, Houghton Mifflin, and Perseus Publishing. She is currently Senior Director of Publicity at Boston's Da Capo Press, a member of the Perseus Books Group. An experienced promoter of both fiction and nonfiction, Ms. Warren holds a B.S. in English Education from Miami University and an M.F.A. in Creative Writing from Bennington College. This fall, she's teaching a graduate course in book publicity at Emerson College.

February 2004
Reference/Media
Paperback Original
5 1/2 x 8 1/4
$14.00 ($20.95 Canada)
272 pages
ISBN: 0-7867-1275-9

AVAILABLE WHEREVER BOOKS ARE SOLD
OR BY CALLING (800) 788-3223

DISTRIBUTED BY PUBLISHERS GROUP WEST

CARROLL & GRAF, AVALON PUBLISHING GROUP

Original Essays on Book-Related Consumer Sites

Your publicist may be able to arrange for you to write an original essay about your book for the following consumer sites:

Booksense.com (for their VIP—Very Interesting Person—section)

Amazon.com (for their "Delivers" e-mails)

BarnesandNoble.com (they'll link to your essay from your book's main page)

Borders.com (they have some wonderful e-newsletters, with names like "Business Class" for business titles, "Alchemy" for health books—be they mind, body, or spirit, "Romantica" for romance novels and relationship guides, "Lit" for fiction, "Arts & Letters" for literary nonfiction like science, history, and current affairs, and "Tractor Beam" for sci-fi)

Original essays are a good way to get these important online booksellers to give your book some extra play. They often let you write about whatever you want, but are always particularly interested in hearing what inspired you to write the book and any funny stories that happened during the writing process—in other words, anything that takes potential customers behind the scenes and makes them feel connected to you. They also like authors to discuss books they liked or found influential, and to relate their book to what's going on in the news.

Reading Groups

Sometimes referred to as a "book club," a reading group is just what it sounds like—a group of people who reads the same book and gathers to discuss it. While most of these groups select paperbacks because they're more affordable, almost a quarter of all reading group purchases are hardcovers. They look for books that generate dialogue—books that are controversial or particularly poignant, be they fiction or nonfiction. The fiction they select tends to lend itself to multiple interpretations.

According to an MRI (Montgomery Research, Inc.) survey, two percent of all Americans participated in a book club in 2002. That's a lot of people, and a lot of potential sales. Consequently, nowadays, many publishing houses make an effort to market directly to these groups. It's also possible for an author to do so. Step one is to find them, and the best place to look is bookstores, libraries, and community centers. Step two is to send a copy of your book (or, if you can't spare a copy, press material and some reviews) to the people who head them, along with a personal note. If you don't have time to do this outreach—or if you want to supplement your efforts—ask your publisher to consider placing an ad in *Reading Group Choices*. Put out by a company called Paz & Associates (http://www.pazbookbiz.com), this guide is distributed via bookstores, public libraries, and Paz's private list of reading groups, reaching over 100,000 participants.

REACHING OUT TO BOOKSELLERS

Drop-by signings

Drop-bys are visits that authors pay to bookstores to sign stock of their books. These are not "formal" signings—no one queues up to get a personalized copy. Instead, you simply autograph the books. They tend to work best with independent bookstores. It's a good idea to call first rather than just "drop by" so that the store can stock up in preparation for your visit. It's good to do drop-bys for three reasons. One, it's a chance to meet-and-greet the people who can hand-sell your book, mention it in their store newsletter or on their store's website, and make it a "staff pick" (which can get it some extra good shelf space). Two, a book signed is a book sold, because bookstores can't return autographed copies. And three, stores will often sticker signed copies (which calls attention to them) and create displays or special signs for them. It's a great way to get your book off the shelf and onto a front table.

A word of caution: if you don't call first and, lo and behold, the store doesn't have your book, do not throw a fit or make a scene! It's possible they had copies but sold out (and have more on order). It's best to just politely inquire and offer to swing by another day. Also, if the store is particularly busy, it might be best to come back later—a staffer will appreciate you much more when talking with you doesn't cause a lost sale with a browsing customer.

Some wholesalers—like BookPeople in Oakland, California—also like it when authors sign stock. So don't forget to include them in your plans.

Lunches or Dinners with Groups of Key Booksellers

If you're personable and good at making small talk, it might be a good idea for your marketing manager to arrange for you to have lunch or dinner with a bunch of booksellers in a particular city while you're on your tour. This works best in cities where there are a lot of independent bookstores. For example, in Boston, you could share some clam chowder at Legal Seafood with buyers from Wordsworth, Brookline Booksmith, Newtonville Books, Harvard Bookstore, and the Concord Bookshop. Or, in San Francisco, you could dine at Fisherman's Wharf with buyers from Cody's, Kepler's, Books Inc., Book Passage, Rakestraw, Stacey's, and Black Oak. While these stores do compete with each other, somewhat, for customers, they're usually willing to raise the white flag and get together when authors are in town.

If you're headed to Ann Arbor, you might share a meal with folks from Borders since they're headquartered there. Same with Barnes & Noble if you're headed to New York, or Amazon.com if you're going to Seattle. For maximum impact, visit these three before they place their orders—which means several months in advance of your book's pub.

Attending Trade Shows

Each spring, booksellers and publishers gather for a national convention called BEA (Book Expo America). It's a chance for the stores to see what titles will be hot for Fall—publishing's biggest season. Members of the media also attend, as do foreign publishers. My authors always ask me whether they should go. The answer is usually no. Unless you're a household name, you'll have a hard time attracting attention in a gigantic hall full of people dressed up as kids' book characters. Famous authors do signings in their publishers' booths or in a special staging area. Some of them are even invited to give special talks as part of the show's official program. But by and large, Joe Average author just comes away completely bewildered—by how many books will pub in competition with his, and by the fact that a lot of the attendees seem much more interested in getting a free poster or tote bag than hearing about a particular title. That said, it is important that your book (provided it's recent or forth-coming) be represented at the show—either by having a display copy available, or by having ARCs for people to take. If your book is a Fall pub, it might even get a lightbox (an illuminated poster that's part of the booth display).

Much less overwhelming are the regional trade shows. They're always held in the Fall. Like BEA, they have publisher booths and chances for authors to speak and sign. The difference—you don't have to be a superstar to get some good attention. The regional book trade shows include:

NEBA (New England Bookseller's Association)
NCIBA (Northern California Independent Bookseller's Association)
SEBA (Southeast Booksellers Association)
NAIBA (New Atlantic Independent Booksellers Association)
PNBA (Pacific Northwest Booksellers Association)
GLBA (Great Lakes Booksellers Association)
MPBA (Mountains and Plains Booksellers Association)
UMBA (Upper Midwest Booksellers Association)
MSIBA (Mid-South Independent Booksellers Association)

If you'd like to participate in one of these shows, speak with your book's marketing manager to see what options exist. Realize that, if you speak or sign, it means your publisher will have to donate at least a hundred books or ARCs—the trade shows do not buy them.

If you think your book will have particular appeal to libraries, make sure it's represented at ALA—the national convention of the American Library Association. It's similar in scope to BEA (not quite as big—but bigger than a regional), so I only advise authors to attend if they're a household name. If your book will appeal to the religious market, you may want to look into attending the CBA (Christian Booksellers Association) convention.

A Book Sense Push

About five years ago, a program called Book Sense was launched in an effort to help independent bookstores compete with the chains and online stores. More than 1,200 stores across America now participate in Book Sense. In addition to having a great Web site (http://www.booksense.com) and putting out the occasional category-specific bestseller list (humor, poetry, parenting, reference, gardening, business, cookbooks, etc.), Book Sense puts out a weekly bestseller list that runs in a number of newspapers and every two months selects seventy-six books that are worthy of special attention. Known as the "Book Sense 76"—after 1776, the year of America's independence—they are featured in a special brochure that goes out to stores in large quantities so that they can be snagged by customers looking for reading recommendations. The top ten titles on the 76 list are also printed in a number of literary publications and go out to tons of bookstores via e-newsletters like *PW Daily* and *Publishers Lunch*. On one occasion, I even saw the top five titles in *USA Today*. In addition, a Book Sense selection provides your publisher with some opportunities for group ads in publications like *The New Yorker* and the *Atlantic Monthly*.

In order to make the Book Sense 76 list, you have to be nominated by participating bookstores—the more of them, the better. In order for this to happen they need to read your book, which means your book's marketing manager needs to send a bound galley or an ARC—or at least a finished book—to as many buyers as possible, with a letter requesting a nomination. They can do this as their own mailing, or they can have it included in Book Sense's bimonthly "white box mailing" (which is just what it sounds like—a big white box full of galleys, T-shirts, bookmarks, and other book-related items). It's hard for a marketing manager to justify printing an extra 1,200 copies for this kind of push, so many only do enough to send to the top 250 or so stores (if sent through Book Sense, it's then known as a "*partial* white box mailing.") And if even 250 sounds high, your book's marketing manager can participate in a program called "Advance Access" in which Book Sense sends an e-mail to all 1,200 stores telling them that the first twenty-five or fifty people to reply that they'd like a galley will receive one.

If your marketing manager thinks your book is a particularly good contender for the Book Sense 76 list, he or she may even follow up with some calls or e-mails to the stores on its behalf, urging them to nominate it. What makes a book a good contender? Book Sense 76 titles are usually quite literary—novels, short story collections, collections of poetry, biographies and memoirs. Rarely do business books make the 76. Same with books on health and parenting, and reference books in general. Science books stand a decent shot so long as they're for the layperson. History can do pretty well. Current affairs, too. If your book falls into one of these categories, encourage the marketing department to try for a selection. If they seem short on time, ask if you can help by drafting the letter or e-mail. You may also want to offer to autograph the bound galleys, ARCs, or finished books.

Sending Personal Letters to Booksellers

It never hurts for an author to send personal letters to key booksellers across the country—including those in your own backyard—telling them about your book and asking for their support. You can do it in the months before your book comes out when the stores are placing their orders, but I think it's more effective to hold off until pub date. Then, you'll have some reviews to include, and maybe a profile piece.

If there's no Book Sense push for your book, you might also want to include an autographed ARC or finished book with your letter.

Chapter 10

The Art of the Pitch

As I've mentioned previously, I discourage authors from pitching the media directly. If you're unhappy with the amount or quality of coverage that your in-house publicist has been able to secure, I strongly advise you to enlist the services of a freelance publicist. That said, I realize not everyone can afford to hire out. For those of you who decide it's necessary to take matters into your own hands, you may as well put your best foot forward. This chapter will help you do that.

Whether it's by phone or by e-mail, by letter or by fax, pitching the media is an art, not a science. As such, it's hard to teach. If you're like me, a lot of what you learn about approaching the media you'll learn by doing. Below are guidelines to help you through the process.

WHAT TO SAY

When you're pitching your book to the media, the best thing you can do is try to put yourself in their shoes. These people are inundated with ideas for guests and articles and reviews. At the same time as they're vetting suggestions and combing through possibilities, they have to prep for the guests they've already booked, or write up the articles for which they've already interviewed people, or edit the reviews that the freelancers have already turned in (late). In addition to these "usual" activities, many members of the media are slaves to breaking news. Their bosses expect them to spin on a dime anytime there's a big court ruling or a celebrity arrest.

What I'm saying is these people are busy. That means you need to keep your pitch short. And since members of the media are by definition skeptics, you need to keep it honest. Producers and the like have great "b.s." detectors, so hype won't get you very far. They don't need to hear that your book is great; they need to hear what makes it great and what ideas you have to offer.

Which leads me to a crucial tip—perhaps the best one in this book. When you are pitching your book to the media, no matter who it is, no matter who you are, you want to pitch them an *idea*. As crazy as it sounds, you don't want to pitch them a book. Never say, "I want to come on your show to talk about my book, *Sonic Boom*, which looks at how Napster is destroying the music industry." Always say, "I want to come on to talk about Napster and the way it's destroying the music industry. I'm the author of a new book on the topic. It's called *Sonic Boom*." It's a subtle difference, but it'll make a big one. It focuses on what you can do for them and on your credentials to do so, rather than what they can do for you.

WHOM TO SAY IT TO

Newsrooms are crazy places, so it's best not to count on a random member of the media to pass your thoughts on to someone who might be able to do something with them. It happens sometimes, to be sure. But not often enough. The most direct path to publicity is through the person responsible for assigning the kind of coverage you're seeking. Following are the people you need to contact for each type of coverage that you're likely to receive.

Book Review Editors

Most major-market newspapers employ someone with the title "Book Review Editor" (a.k.a. "Books Editor"). This is the person you want to persuade to assign your book for review, usually in their Sunday "Books" section, though some papers like the *Boston Globe* and *New York Times* also run daily reviews (note: the *Wall Street Journal* and *USA Today* only run reviews on weekdays, since they don't have Sunday editions). In some instances—for lead books or at a smaller paper—the Book Review Editor may write the review himself. More often, they'll assign the piece to a freelance reviewer or a writer who's on staff (for example, they might assign a book on the history of Louisiana blues to their music critic, or a biography of Richard Feynman to their science editor). The Book Review Editor may also serve as a clearing house for other sections of the publication. For example, while they may not review many parenting or health books, they may regularly pass these volumes along to their parenting columnist or their health reporter, who may have use for them. At some publications, the Book Review Editor is also the right person to approach for off-the-book-page coverage like a profile piece about you, or perhaps a Q&A. At other publications, these types of articles are handled by features editors. Their sections are often called things like "Living," "Life," "Style," or "Lifestyle." At larger papers, you might also find someone with the title "Deputy Books Editor." They're sometimes more receptive to an author than "the boss."

As for magazines, most national ones also have a "Book Review Editor." They serve the same function they do at the papers—assigning reviews, occasionally writing them, and passing books on to other sections.

Why do some books get assigned for review while others are passed up? If publishers knew the answer to that question, life would be a lot easier! Alas, selecting books for review seems to be a rather subjective process, sometimes based as much on the personal interests of the Book Review Editor (or his perception of the interests of his readers) as anything else. For example, you'll see the *New York Times Book Review* cover an unusually large number of books on golf and baseball. Why? Because editor Chip McGrath is a big fan of both and his status in the literary world affords him the security to indulge his personal passions.

But there are some things that Book Review Editors are always on the watch for. For nonfiction titles, they want the author to be an authority in his or her field (yet able to write for the intelligent layperson). For fiction, they gravitate toward first-time novelists— especially young ones whom they want the distinction of having "discovered"—and well-established authors whom they'd look foolish not to review. So authors who could be "the next big thing" and institutions like Updike and Roth have it pretty good when it comes to reviews.

What can you or your publicist do to convince a Book Review Editor to assign your book? One thing that helps is a positive review in one or, even better, *several* of the four bellweather publications in the publishing world: *Booklist, Library Journal, Kirkus Reviews,* and *Publishers Weekly.* Running pre-pub, reviews in these publications really influence decisions—both for bookstores and libraries (in terms of what they buy) and for media (in terms of what they will review). I cannot overstate the importance of getting your book reviewed in these "advance review" publications. If the reviews are favorable, be sure to mail or fax or e-mail them to all of the Book Review Editors to whom galleys were sent. If they run prior to the finished book mailing, be sure to include them in your finished book press material. And if a pre-pub review is "starred" (meaning it's been called it out with some sort of asterisk—the trades do this for the books they really like), be sure to always refer to it as such. I remember sitting in the office of *Business Week*'s Book Review Editor, Hardy Green, asking him what it would take to convince him a particular title was worthy of a review. "Did it get a starred *PW?*" he asked. Alas, that time, I was not able to say it had.

Book Critics

Some newspapers also have what's called a "Book Critic." Some of the most well-known include Gail Caldwell (*Boston Globe*), Jonathan Yardley (*Washington Post*), David Kipen (*San Francisco Chronicle*), Carlin Romano (*Philadelphia Inquirer*), and Deirdre Donahue and Bob Minzesheimer (*USA Today*). Never one to be outdone, the "Paper of Record" (known to us all as the *New York Times*) has four—Richard Eder, Janet Maslin, Richard Bernstein, and Michiko Kakutani. These are the people who review books for the paper each week. They have a "steady gig," as it were. They also have a lot of influence. Some of them even choose what they want to review, rather than having it assigned to them. If yours is the kind of book that's appropriate for review, you want to make sure these individuals have been sent copies. As for following up, don't do it. These folks will barely tolerate publicist's calls, let alone calls from authors. As *USA Today*'s Minzesheimer put it in a September 2002 Salon.com article, "I always think if I'm hearing directly from the author, it's not a good sign." In the same piece, the *Washington Post*'s Yardley put it more bluntly: "I really, really, really don't like authors to contact me."

Some magazines also have a Book Critic—for example, Sven Birkerts at *Esquire* and John Leonard at *Harper's*.

Special Book Review Editors

Some papers also have people (both on-staff and freelance) who review books, or assign books for review, within a particular section (not the books section). For example, Steve Powers reviews business books in the *Dallas Morning News*'s "Business" section as does economics reporter Steve Pearlstein in the *Washington Post*. Richard Pachter assigns them at the *Miami Herald* (he even does a business "book club" with one selection per month), as does Bill Castle at the *Boston Globe* and Jacqui Blais at *USA Today* (for their

"Money" section). At the *Columbus Dispatch*, George Myers reviews technology books in his weekly "Connect" section. Some papers also have very book-friendly columnists. At the *San Diego Union-Tribune*, Scott Lafee often reviews science books in his "Eureka" column. Recently, the *Boston Globe* has started reviewing health and science books in their Tuesday "Health/Science" section (the assigning editor is Karen Weintraub). At *Newsday*, Jamie Talan briefly reviews health and science books in her "In the Mix" column. At the *Minneapolis Star Tribune*, H. J. Cummings reviews parenting books in her column. The best way to find these columnists is via the web. A week or two of banging around the *Nashville Tennessean*'s site will acquaint you with Beth Stein, who frequently uses her column to review parenting and women's-issues books (with a shot of the book's cover—in color, no less).

Radio Producers/TV Producers

Authors often think the way to get onto a TV or radio show is to send a book to the host or anchor. This seems to make sense. You hear or see these personalities on the air and you get a good feel, you think, for what might interest them. And sometimes sending books to them works, especially with people like Peter Jennings of ABC *Nightly News* who are very involved in selecting what gets covered. But those people are tough to follow up with. For sure-fire results, you want to send to one of the show's producers instead (unless you have a personal relationship with the host; that's another matter entirely). Some radio and TV shows have an official "Books Producer," and they're usually your best bet. For example, all three morning shows have a person with this title (Kristin Matthews at CBS's *Early Show*, Patty Neger at ABC's *Good Morning America*, and Andrea Smith at NBC's *Today Show*). The evening newsmagazine shows have them too (Jackie Levin at *Dateline*, Diana

Pierce at Nightline, Trish Arico at 20/20) as do talk shows like Charlie Rose (Courtney Litz) and Larry King (Mercedes Torres). At NPR's Fresh Air, Amy Salit handles all the books. At NPR's Diane Rehm, it's Elizabeth Terry's job. At Marketplace, which airs on PRI (Public Radio International), all books should go to Heidi Pickman. For shows that don't have someone who is specifically responsible for books—like most local radio and TV shows—you can deal with any producer. Some shows divvy up producing responsibility by subject matter (for example, they may have one producer who handles sports coverage, one who handles politics, one who handles science). In that case, send to the appropriate person for your category. You can often find these people via the Web, or by making a call to the station. Some radio and TV stations also post their producers' bios on their Web site, sometimes with personal information like their college major, their hobbies, the number of kids they have, and the type of pets. This is a great way to ascertain their personal interests and to target (and tailor) your pitch accordingly.

Two final tips for pitching radio and TV producers: never call them the hour before their show (they'll be dealing with last-minute preparations and cancellations, breaking news, etc.) and never tell a producer you'll only be on their show to talk about a certain subject if they have you on at a later date to talk about your book (they resent being blackmailed and if you're good, they'll invite you back to discuss your book anyway).

Reporters/Columnists

Are you an avid reader of Redbook's "Mommy Strategies" column? Do you go nuts over Chet Raymo's "Science Musings" column in the Boston Globe, or Charlie Stein's "Economic Principles" column in the same paper? Are you a fan of Dr. Drew Pinsky's sex-ed column in USA Weekend magazine, or Dan Savage's ultra-explicit "Savage Love" column that runs in alternative papers like the *Village Voice*, or Bob Rosner's "Working Wounded" business column which appears in the *Los Angeles Times* as well as on ABCnews.com? All of these columns mention books from time to time—and sometimes even build columns around them. And columnists often welcome suggestions from authors. So do reporters, especially when they're looking for experts who can comment on the news or whose books can be used as a springboard to an article. For example, if you've written a book about the detrimental effects of genetically modified food and a new study comes out that shows genetically modified corn is harmful to monarch butterflies, you're just the kind of person environmental reporters at the major-market dailies and the newsweeklies (*Newsweek, Time, U.S. News & World Report*, etc.) will be wanting to talk with. So get in touch with them . . . and pronto before someone else does. If you've written a book about how to use the Web to manage your money, send it to personal finance editors as well as technology reporters. If you've authored a diet book, send it to people who cover health and fitness. You get the idea. And you won't find it hard to track these folks down. A call to the paper or mag should do the trick, or hit their sites for the mastheads. Just remember never to call a newspaper reporter after 3:00 P.M. (he'll be on deadline, and in no mood to talk).

WHEN TO SAY IT

The Initial Approach

So when should you approach the media about your book? Most radio and TV producers can wait for finished books, the exception being the evening newsmagazines, which start planning early for each show, and the morning shows and nationally syndicated shows on NPR (National Public Radio), which book up fast because competition is fierce. But the Book Review Editors at newspapers and magazines (including the four key advance ones: *Publishers Weekly, Kirkus Reviews, Library Journal,* and *Booklist*) will definitely need to receive a bound galley of your book three to four months before it hits stores—more like four to six months if it's a Book Review Editor at a monthly magazine that has a long lead time (for example, *Fast Company, Discover, Self, Cosmo, Glamour, Seventeen, Parents, Parenting, Child*). If you don't have galleys in time or if you're not doing galleys for your book, send a bound manuscript. You can have them tape-bound at local copy shops like Kinko's or Copy Cop (hint: if you have access to a copy machine and want to save money, do the copying yourself and just have the shop do the binding). You can also bind your manuscript yourself with rings or posts, though they're not the media's preferred method (if you decide to go this route, you can buy the paper with the holes already punched so that you don't have to punch them yourself). Regardless of the method you use, be sure to include the book's cover as the front page of any bound manuscript (preferably in color, but black-and-white is much cheaper and will suffice). Also be sure that somewhere on the manuscript it lists your contact information, the book's pubdate, and the name of the house that's publishing it.

As for off-the-book-page coverage in newspapers—mentions in columns, feature pieces, etc.—you can generally wait and send the finished book. For off-the-book-page coverage in magazines, you'll need to send a galley three to four months in advance—or, even better, a bound manuscript four to six months in advance.

Follow-Up

Around the time your galley or bound manuscript hits their desks, you want to reach out to the people to whom you sent it. I usually find e-mail is best for this. The phone is good, too (in which case I sometimes place my calls after hours or on weekends so that I'm sure to get voice mail, which enables me to convey the information I need to without forcing the contact to drop what he's doing).

Regardless of how you're conducting your follow-up—but especially if it's via phone during business hours when you might actually get a real live (working) human being—best not to say something like, "Did you receive the galley I sent?" The media gets annoyed by that question because they get a ton of galleys, and often can't say which ones they have and haven't received. Your asking puts them in an awkward spot (plus it sounds a little silly; if you sent it, chances are they got it—unless the little green mail demons beat them to it). Better to say something like, "You should have just received a galley for my book *The Best Book in the World*. I just wanted to call your attention to it. It's a June pub, and it's a history of X (or a memoir of X, or a critical look at X)." I sometimes even describe the galley in the hope it'll help them locate it in their stacks ("It's a bright green galley with a picture of X on the front," or "It has a purple spine"). I always end by saying something like, "If you're unable to locate the copy I sent, just let me know and I'll be happy to send another." Don't forget to provide your phone number.

During the time between your first follow-up after receipt of the galley or bound manuscript and your follow-up after you send the finished book, you should plan on communicating with each recipient another time or two—or even three—to make sure your book is being seriously considered. During these communications, you should mention any favorable advance reviews your book receives (quote the review or send it in its entirety; if it was a *starred* review be sure to indicate that as it can make a major difference). For the major-market dailies, you should remind them of any talks you'll be giving in their area. It increases the chance that they'll run a review and that it will coincide with your talk, which would help to drive folks to the event.

When your book comes off press and you do your big mailing of finished copies to the media, that's when your publicity effort can really kick into gear. That's when you'll want to start reaching out for off-the-book-page coverage in newspapers. That's when you'll want to start pitching the remaining radio and TV.

When to Move On

Of course, the corollary to when to start talking with the media about your book is when to *stop* talking about it. A publicist friend of mine once told me that she follows up with the media until she gets a yes or a no. Another publicist friend once said her rule's "three strikes, you're out"—meaning she contacts each member of the media three times about each book, and then moves on. Most times, I fall somewhere in the middle. For a small show or publication, or one you feel probably isn't quite right for your book, you may only want to follow up with them once or twice (for example, once as a chaser to the galley; once as a chaser to the finished book). For a show or publication that you know is key to your book's success—e.g., the *New York Times Book Review* or *Oprah*—and if you truly feel your book is right for coverage there, you might want to try a dozen or more times, with a few different people at each. Some things are really worth fighting for.

THE FIVE METHODS OF PITCHING

When pitching your book to the media, there are five different methods to use:

Phone

Okay, I'll admit it. This is, by far, the most intimidating way of reaching out to the media. It took me years to get used to it.

However, if you're quick on your feet, it can also be one of the most effective ways to influence them. It provides you with the opportunity to hear what's keeping someone from writing about your book or having you on their show, and the chance to counter their arguments and change their mind. Case in point, I was recently on the phone with a producer at Fox News's *Your World with Neil Cavuto* about a book of ours called *The Great 401(k) Hoax*. The producer said to me, "I'm sorry, but we don't cover personal finance titles on this show." I explained to her that it's actually a book about the economic history of the 401(k) and a prediction of how it will put future generations in peril. I said it wasn't "an advice book" but rather "a book that's 'big-think.' " The whole thing took about thirty seconds. She agreed to take another look at it, and called back the next day to book an interview with the author.

So how do you start the conversation when you get someone on the phone? Assuming you've already sent them the book, you might say something like this to a radio or TV producer: "Hi. This is Jane Doe. I'd like to come on your show to talk about the trend in X (or the rise in X in America, or ways to keep your family safe from X), and am calling to see whether you might be interested. I'm the author of a new book called *Examining X*, a copy of which I sent your way a week ago." The ideal response: "Why yes, I have the book sitting right here and have been meaning to call you. Let's schedule an interview for tomorrow." The more likely response: "*Examining X*? Haven't seen it. Doesn't ring a bell." In that case, you can do one of two things, depending on their tone. You can launch into your pitch right then and there ("The book looks at the various ways corporate America puts the average consumer at risk and offers solutions to this escalating problem—solutions that range from A to Z.") or you can offer to e-mail or fax them press material for the book. (Note: if they ask you to mail them another copy of your book instead, be sure to mark the package REQUESTED

MATERIAL; it increases the chance they'll look at it). Regardless, expect to have to follow up with them again in a week or so. If they don't call you, it doesn't mean they're not interested.

But what do you say when the producer asks, "So when will you be in New York?" (or D.C. or LA—wherever the show is based)? The answer is easy if you're headed to that city. If you're not, here's what you do: if it's TV, suggest linking up from the affiliate nearest you. If it's radio, ask if they do phoners (if not, suggest going to a radio studio near you). Be prepared for them to say, "Sorry, you'd have to come here." There are some shows that require that, and then you have a choice to make—namely, whether it's worth the cost of travel. If it's a national show, I'm inclined to say it is.

Here's another scenario: say you're going to Austin in three weeks to do a talk at the independent bookstore Book People and you want to do an interview on Austin's NPR affiliate while you're in town. You've hit their Web site and have found a show that sounds right for your book, but you can't tell who produces it. The best thing to do is call the general number for the station and press zero for the operator. Tell her you're calling to get the name of the person who produces the "X" show, then ask her to transfer you to that person. When they pick up, say something along the lines of "Hi. This is Jane Doe. I'll be in Austin in three weeks for a talk at BookPeople, and would like to come on your show to talk about X. I'm the author of a new book called *Examining X*. May I fax or e-mail you some more information?" Again, expect to have to follow up.

Likewise, if you're heading to Austin and want to get coverage in the *Austin American-Statesman*, hit their Web site and see who writes about the topic to which you can speak. Call them or the Book Review Editor and pitch a story (be sure to tell them you'll be in town for a talk so that they know there's a local hook). You might be able to wrangle an in-person interview while you're there (or, better yet, an interview via phone before you get there so the piece can run a day or two before your event).

Voice Mail

Should you leave a voice mail message for a member of the media? I don't generally find voice mail effective for initial pitches (the media tends to resent having their voice mail clogged up and some editors, reporters, and producers even have messages asking you not to do it). But if your goal is to simply give them a reminder about your book, absolutely. Voice mail is perfect for follow-up.

If you're seeking to obtain information from the media—for example, whether or not your book has been assigned for review—voice mail's probably not the best method (they're generally lousy about calling back with this kind of info). Instead, I recommend ringing the Book Review Editor until you actually get him or her on the phone. Or try e-mail.

Obviously, when you do leave a voice mail message, it's important to keep it short. You don't want to get cut off; they don't want to hear you ramble. But the most important thing is to make sure your message contains the key facts: your name as well as the name of your book, what it's about (one sentence will do), the fact that you've sent it their way (if you have), the fact that you'll be in town (if you will), and, of course, your phone number (so many folks forget that, and it's the most important part; be sure to say it slowly—I usually repeat it).

E-mail

Ah, e-mail. God's gift to authors. It's true that e-mails are easy to ignore and often viewed as a bit informal, but they're also the best way to correspond with the media. They're fast. They're easy. There's something almost anonymous about them so you don't feel like you're intruding on the media and they don't feel like they have to lie to you if they're not interested. They can get you a "yes" or a "no" or a "maybe" so that you know where you stand. The media won't call you back to reject you, but sometimes they will hit "reply" and then "send."

E-mail is also great because it provides the best of both worlds: it can get you a quick response but offers you time to craft your pitch and get it perfect. Nerves may keep you from saying what you mean to say on the phone, but e-mail lets you be thoughtful, and purposeful, and eloquent. An author on e-mail is a fish in water—you're in your element; writing's what you do.

Should you e-mail your whole press release? That's why God created attachments! Should you provide links to reviews or to your Web site? Absolutely, yes, you bet. Make full use of your ammo; e-mail's great for that. And be sure the subject line contains the title of your book so the media can locate it without a lot of effort.

What should you say in your e-mail? The cardinal rule is to make sure it doesn't look like spam, or like something you've sent to a dozen other media contacts. If, for example, you're e-mailing a radio producer, you might try something like this:

Dear Ms. Jones:

I'd very much like to discuss the myriad benefits of yoga on (*insert name of show*). I'm the author of *The Best Yoga Book in the World,* a copy of which I sent your way a week ago (let me know if you didn't receive it and would like me to re-send). If you're interested, perhaps we could time my appearance to the National Institute of Health's new study on yoga. The results will be released a week from Monday.

I've attached a press release for the book and have pasted in quotes from some of the reviews. *Shape* magazine is running an excerpt from the book in its October issue, and a Q&A with me appears in the September issue of *Yoga Journal*. Here's a link: *http://www.yogajournal.com/BestYogaBookQ&A.*

Best,
John Smith
(212) 555-1234

Mail

What courier should you use to send someone your manuscript, galley, or book? It all depends on how quickly he needs it, and how much you're willing to spend. I usually send via U.S. mail—priority if it needs to get there quickly (it usually takes two to three days, and costs a little over three bucks for an average-size book) or media mail (formerly known as "book rate," a.k.a. "slow boat to China"). Media mail can take two to three weeks, but cuts the cost by approximately half. UPS Ground is another choice, takes three to five days, and costs about the same as priority mail unless you have to send it cross-country, in which case it costs more. But you get a bonus with UPS Ground—a tracking number with which you can trace your package. If you need to overnight something, you have three main options: Fed Ex, UPS Next Day, or U.S. Express Mail. All three of them offer Saturday service (for Fed Ex and UPS it costs extra). If you need to have the package delivered on a Sunday, U.S. Express is your only option, and is not available to all locations.

When I don't use e-mail to send follow-up letters, I use first-class mail—usually with pre-pub reviews. I do this to make a statement; email is cheaper and faster, but easier to overlook.

What should you say in your letters? For starters, keep the text to a page. The tone should be "business casual"—friendly, but not too friendly; informative but not didactic. For example, a follow-up letter to a Book Review Editor might go something like this:

> Dear Mr. Smith,
>
> I've enclosed advance reviews for my book *The Trendiest Book in the World* in the hope they'll convince you to assign it for review if you've not already done so. It looks at the growing trend toward X in America and what this trend says about our culture.
>
> I spent four years researching this book and took another two to write it in the hope that it would capture what we as a nation are striving toward and against. I'd very much like to see my book covered in your pages. A finished copy was sent your way a week or two ago, but if you need another by all means let me know. My e-mail address is jane.doe@janedoe.com and my phone number is (212) 555-1234.
>
> Best,
> Jane Doe

Fax

Oh, dear God, I hate faxing. I never feel confident that my fax goes through. And faxes have a way of getting lost in a newsroom, or crumpled up for kitty litter, or something . . . I don't know. It's simply not a great method to use, unless, of course, you're asked to. If you are, make sure to include a cover sheet with your name, your phone, and the number of pages. Otherwise, I'd mail your correspondence—or shoot along an e-mail.

WHAT *NOT* TO SAY

As I hinted earlier, it's important not to praise your book as part of your pitch. It's the media's job to assess it, not yours. And, as I've already mentioned, you want what you say to focus on what you can do for the media, not what they can do for you. My final word of advice is to be careful to strike a good balance between highlighting the coverage your book has already received and making it sound like it has already been done to death. In the words of a publicist friend who shall remain nameless, "No one likes sloppy seconds." It's fine to tell the *Chicago Sun-Times* that the *Washington Post* has profiled you. It's good to do so, actually—makes you sound like a pretty big deal. But if you tell them your face has recently graced the *Chicago Tribune*, you could be dead in the water. That's their competition, and they don't like to be scooped. (One caveat: if they ask you point-blank whether you've already been covered by the competition, don't lie—one quick search on the Web and you're busted.) Another example: if you tell NPR's *Morning Edition* that *Talk of the Nation* or *All Things Considered* has recently had you on, you're probably not going to need to clear your calendar for another segment anytime soon. Not sure who competes with whom? Best to err on the side of caution when it comes to this kind of thing. If you have a solid pitch, you're not going to need to impress the media with a litany of "already rans" anyway.

Whether it's radio, TV, newspaper, or magazine—by phone, or e-mail, or courier, or fax—pitching the media takes practice. So be patient with yourself as you figure out the very best way to present your book. And if you seem to be hitting brick walls, check out the ideas in the following chapter.

Chapter 11

Ten Things to Do If Your Book's Not Getting Media Attention

When I'm working on a book and it just isn't getting coverage, there are certain steps I take, and certain steps I ask my authors to take. Here are ten of them.

1. HONESTLY ASSESS YOUR BOOK'S MEDIA POTENTIAL.

Has it been done before? Is there lots of competition? While you're at it, assess your own media potential. Are you regarded as an expert in your field? If yours is a science book, are you a scientist? If yours is a book about medicine, are you a doctor? If yours is a business book, are you a CEO at a big corporation? If not, you're likely to find it hard to get interviews. A writer does not an expert make—unless, of course, it's a book about writing. Could you be overexposed? Could your topic be overexposed? If you've written a book about dotcoms or Enron, or a book about boys or mean girls, you're bound to find it a bit of a tough go. But remember, media isn't the only way to make people notice your book.

2. WRITE AN OP-ED TIED TO YOUR BOOK.

When it runs, send it out to all of the broadcast media you've been targeting.

3. TRY TO GET INTERVIEWED FOR SOMETHING OTHER THAN YOUR BOOK.

Not having any luck getting the media to talk with you about your title? See if you can interest them in speaking with you about another topic. For example, if your book focuses on how to lose weight, see if you can get your local paper to do a piece about your award-winning sugar-cookies. Tell them about the irony so that they give a nod to your book. Or if your book is about your memories of high school football but it's baseball season, try to get a sports radio station to have you on to talk about the joys of high school athletics in general. They'll probably still mention the book in your intro.

4. GO READ THE NEWSPAPER OR LISTEN TO NPR.

Try to find current events to which you can gear your pitch. If your book is about job interview techniques and the latest unemployment figures just came out (and have risen), you've got a new hook. If your book is a guide to Atlanta and it's about to be named a top-ten city, call up *USA Today*'s "Destinations & Diversions" section and ask whether they want to interview you for a sidebar to run alongside the rankings.

5. LOOK FOR OTHER NEW BOOKS ON THE SAME TOPIC AS YOURS.

Two books equal a trend, and reporters *love* to do trend pieces. For example, in the Spring of 2002, we published a book called *Linked: The New Science of Networks*. Around the same time, Norton published another book about networks, *Nexus*. By calling this to the attention of science reporters, we were able to get more coverage than we could have gotten with our book alone. Another example: in June of 2002, the *New York Times* ran a big piece about perimenopause that included a bunch of books on the subject along with info on various estrogen supplements.

6. TAKE A LONG, HARD LOOK AT YOUR PRESS MATERIAL.

Is it too hypey? Does it seem outdated in the light of current events? If it's skewed heavily to one section of your book, could you redo it to skew to another section in which the media might take more interest? It's also important to get someone else's take on your press material. While it's true that no one knows your book—or you—the way you do, it's important to get feedback that provides outside perspective.

7. ASSESS WHETHER YOU'RE TARGETING THE RIGHT *KIND* OF MEDIA.

Are you going for media that's too high-brow (or low-brow) for your book? Are you wasting time trying to get *reviews* in major market papers? (If your book is self-help, health, parenting, new-age, or very technical, the answer is probably "yes"; but don't lose heart—those kind of books are great for off-the-book-page coverage.) Are you focusing on long-lead-time magazines after your book is already out? (If so, it's probably too late for them; go for the weekly mags instead.) Be honest with yourself: Do you have the right "sound" for radio? The right "look" for TV?

8. LOOK FOR NEW MEDIA OUTLETS TO APPROACH, ESPECIALLY IN YOUR CITY.

For instance, have you exhausted the following local affiliates: NPR, CBS, ABC, NBC, PBS, Fox? Have you tried the alumni magazine for your college and your grad school? Have you tried your hometown paper for a "local boy makes good" article? Have you tried all the magazines to which you subscribe? To get more ideas, have you gone to a newsstand? Have you approached the websites you surf on a regular basis? What about the drive-time shows on your local FM (and AM) stations? (To find them, just go to Google.com and type in the name of your city with the word "radio" next to it.)

9. EVALUATE THE WAY YOU'RE APPROACHING THE MEDIA.

Are your e-mails not getting answered? Try phoning the media instead. Are your phone messages being ignored? Try e-mailing or faxing.

10. DETERMINE WHETHER YOU'RE USING ALL YOUR AMMO.

Are you including quotes from your reviews and copies of other coverage? Are they presented in an impressive way (in a folder or in color)? Does your bio list the shows you've done and the groups for which you've spoken? If you're touring, does it clearly state the venues where you're speaking so that each city's media know there's a local hook?

Any one of these ten steps can help you save your book—can help you get it the attention it deserves. Like all of the tips in *The Savvy Author's Guide to Book Publicity*, they're meant to encourage you to think like the pros. But the most important thing is to keep a positive attitude. You are, after all, a published author; you've already accomplished what very few have done. Good luck as you embark on this journey. May it be meaningful, and fun.

APPENDIX

There are various types of press material you can create (or help your publicist create). Here are some samples you can draw from, a few in final form and others in a more readable format:

GALLEY LETTERS
Recommended Length: I Page

Stillwater Press
712 POND STREET · CAMBRIDGE, MASSACHUSETTS · 02142
ph. 617.555.1234 · *fx.* 555.5678 · W W W.STILLWATERPRESS.COM

November 28, 2000

Dear Editor / Reporter / Producer:

It's especially common among young women. In fact, it may affect up to ten percent of the female population, though most of us don't know we have it. There's no way to prevent it, and ignoring it can result in everything from minor discomfort to gangrene. What is this mysterious illness, and what can be done about it?

In *Cold Hands, Warm Heart: A Guide to Living with Raynaud's*, noted rheumatologist Dr. Kay Stackpole sheds light on Raynaud's disease—a widely experienced condition in which blood supply to the fingers and toes—and sometimes even the ears and nose—is interrupted due to a contraction of the arteries brought about by exposure to cold. During an attack, the affected extremity becomes white, then red, and eventually blue as it warms, before returning to its normal color. Pain, numbness, and tingling usually accompany each episode.

A practical guide, *Cold Hands, Warm Heart* is peppered with personal stories of women living with Raynaud's, including Dr. Stackpole herself. She shares tips derived from three decades of Chicago winters while spelling out how Raynaud's is diagnosed and clarifying the difference between the two types of the disease. There's a chapter on the dangers of Raynaud's—such as its association with Scleroderma, lupus, Sjögrens syndrome, and rheumatoid arthritis—as well as a chapter on the latest treatment options.

Complete with an appendix full of resources for further information and support, *Cold Hands, Warm Heart* is a "must-have" for anyone recently diagnosed with Raynaud's and anyone who has been living with the disease but who doesn't feel she has "mastered" it—someone in search of advice, not just facts.

Dr. Kay Stackpole is a prominent Chicago rheumatologist and a Raynaud's sufferer herself. Her research into biofeedback's effects on Raynaud's have revolutionized the treatment of the disease. She lives with her husband in Oak Park, Illinois.

I'm pleased to enclose a galley for *Cold Hands, Warm Heart*, which we'll publish in February of 2001. Should you need any further information or should you wish to arrange an interview with Dr. Stackpole, please don't hesitate to contact me at (617) 555-1234 or via e-mail at calla.mckittrick@stillwaterpress.com.

Best,

Calla McKittrick
Director of Publicity

Stillwater Press

712 Pond Street, Cambridge, Massachusetts 02142

(617) 555-1234 ph. / (617) 555-5678 fx.

www.stillwaterpress.com

> "Long after the bell had rung—long after Pastor Wayne set out
> to find his lost black sheep—Elspeth was still thinking about
> what she had learned: That grace is getting what you don't deserve,
> and mercy's not getting what you do; that sex would smell
> like woodsmoke; that the human body freezes, and the human
> body melts."
>
> —from "The Pastor's Son"

June 14, 2001

Dear Editor/Reporter/Producer:

I'm pleased to enclose a galley for Mahlia Gerald's debut collection
The Men She Slept With, which we'll publish in October as a paperback
original.

All of the stories in *The Men She Slept With* center around a naive but
oddly intuitive young woman known simply as Elspeth. In "The
Pastor's Son," we see her struggle to reconcile lust with the Christian
faith as she spends a winter weekend on a co-ed church retreat. Later,
in "Caddy Shack-Up," she first becomes aware of the power of her own
sexuality, only to see it squandered by a boy who opts instead for a
"sure thing." The fifth story, "The Lord's Motel," takes us to Key West
where Elspeth visits Hemingway's house and falls for a man who writes
in his sleep. The penultimate story, "The Champagne Headache,"
brings us to Rome where Elspeth gets drunk and shares her bed with
a man who has left her. And finally, in "Tangles," we learn of Elspeth's

brief affair with a doctor who's out to cure Alzheimer's—a man who leads her to the hopeful conclusion that "love, like the plaques in the brain, can erase every man you've ever slept with."

Throughout Gerald's collection, we are reminded of the fact that sleeping beside someone can be far more intimate than sleeping with them, that sex and faith can coexist, and love cannot be forced or fostered. A book that heralds the arrival of a brave and brazen new voice in fiction, *The Men She Slept With* promises to keep us awake late into the night.

Mahlia Gerald's work has appeared in such publications as *Agni*, *Ploughshares*, and *Glimmer Train*. She holds an M.F.A. in Creative Writing from Sarah Lawrence College and lives in a western suburb of Cleveland where she teaches high school English. Ms. Gerald's tour for *The Men She Slept With* will take place the last two weeks of October and will consist of events in Cleveland, Columbus, Cincinnati, Chicago, Boston, New York, D.C., and Philadelphia. For further information or to schedule an interview with the author, please don't hesitate to contact me at (617) 555-1234 or via e-mail at calla.mckittrick@stillwaterpress.com.

Best,

Calla McKittrick
Director of Publicity

Stillwater Press

712 Pond Street, Cambridge, Massachusetts 02142

(617) 555-1234 ph. / (617) 555-5678 fx.

www.stillwaterpress.com

March 3, 2003

Dear Editor/Reporter/Producer:

As horticulturists across the United States begin to plan their summer gardens, I'm pleased to enclose a galley for Susan Castor's *Lilac Rogue*—the first biography of Ian MacLaughlin, the man who "invented" the lilac.

In 1832, MacLaughlin, then President of the Botanical Society of the Republic (which went on to become the American Horticultural Society in 1922) and a scientist by profession, created the lilac in a primitive lab by crossing the lily of the valley with a now-extinct bush. The reaction from the botanical community was instant and brutal; they shunned MacLaughlin for "bastardizing nature," believing that "ground cover" should not be mixed with "trees." In a unanimous vote, he was ousted from his post.

MacLaughlin would fight back. The following year, he began engaging in acts of "botanical sabotage," infesting the gardens of his neighbors with beetles, "poisoning" plants at a rose competition, and setting fire to the greenhouse of the Society's new head. When his wife of two decades learned what he was up to, he left her for his brother's mistress and assumed a new identity in France. Three years later, he would be arrested for selling a "priceless" red hydrangea that was, in reality, a white one dyed in a cask of Bordeaux.

At once a biography of a troubled and passionate man and a tribute to America's most literary flower (think Whitman's "When Lilacs Last in the Dooryard Bloom'd" and Dickinson's "Upon a Lilac Sea"), *Lilac Rogue* takes its place alongside Karl Sabbagh's *A Rum Affair* and other classics of botanical fraud.

Susan Castor is Director of the New York Botanical Garden and a frequent contributor to *Horticulture* magazine. She spent seventeen years researching MacLaughlin in preparation for this book. She lives in the Park Slope section of Brooklyn with her husband and daughter.

We'll publish *Lilac Rogue* on June 14th, the official start of "Lilac Season." For further information or to schedule an interview with the author, please don't hesitate to contact me at (617) 555-1234 phone, (617) 555-5678 fax, or via e-mail at calla.mckittrick@stillwaterpress.com.

Best,

Calla McKittrick
Director of Publicity

PRESS RELEASES
(HARDCOVERS AND PAPERBACK ORIGINALS)
Recommended Length: 1–2 Pages

Stillwater Press

712 POND STREET · CAMBRIDGE, MASSACHUSETTS · 02142
ph. 617.555.1234 · *fx.* 555.5678 · WWW.STILLWATERPRESS.COM

Contact: Calla McKittrick, Director of Publicity
(617) 555-1234 / calla.mckittrick@stillwaterpress.com

The Want of Rain
Poems

By JUDSON KELL

The opening section of Judson Kell's second collection of poetry, *The Want of Rain,* explores the tenuous but profound connection between art and place, taking us from Cezanne's home in the hills of Aix to the Kentucky farm of Kell's childhood where "there, still, in lead on the wall/ is 'drain three feet north from pear tree.' " Later, in poems like "Heron" and "Brood," Kell turns his attention to relationships—those that nurture, those that destroy, and those that ultimately define us: "Say what you saw I am to you:/ dross and a communion host,/ someone to sift, a moment's rest."

In "Pigeons in Sleet"—the final section of *The Want of Rain*—Kell examines the role of desire in our lives: desire for love, desire for acceptance, and the desire to somehow "chisel the night" that is our own demise. With a clear eye and a knack for understatement, he hones in on that which makes us human—"a room in a museum made of flowers made of glass/ the hope that what we've cut can last."

Judson Kell is a 1996 graduate of the Iowa Writer's Workshop. His poems have appeared in *Poetry,* the *American Poetry Review, Poetry Northwest, Bloomsbury Review,* and numerous other publications. A professor of creative writing at Merrimack College, he lives in Andover, Massachusetts, with his wife, the painter Dora Westmead. His previous collection of poetry, *The Horse Wanted Sugar,* was published by Absinthe Press in 1998.

April 1, 2003 • Poetry • Hardcover • 96 Pages •
$17.50 • ISBN: 0-1234-5678-9

"Kell is to be commended for his steadfast commitment to the lyric poem in an age when it is tragically undervalued. In this, his second volume of verse, he does not disappoint."
—*Publishers Weely* (starred review)

"The section entitled 'The Calla's Throat' alone is worth the price of the book."
—*Booklist* (starred review)

"Kell's poems, 'Livebearers' and 'Still the City Is Your Body' chief among them, remid us of the adage 'no poetry but in things.' He is an imagist working a lyric tradition, and for that pairing we owe him thanks." —*Library Journal*

"Succulent...Kell displays a steady hand." —*Kirkus Reviews*

Stillwater Press

712 Pond Street, Cambridge, Massachusetts 02142

(617) 555-1234 ph. / (617) 555-5678 fx.

www.stillwaterpress.com

November 28, 2000

Contact: Calla McKittrick, Director of Publicity
(617) 555-1234 / calla.mckittrick@stillwaterpress.com

"He watched her dance around the candles, her long skirt snuffing many out while making others flare. Later, he would yell at her for tracking in the wax. But for now he stood there as she wound her way toward him, her neck impossibly long, her wrists making tiny clockwise dips as if to say 'do not let time be wasted.' "

—from Chapter Two, "The Feast of San Gennaro"

Terpsichore's Muse
A Novel
by **Nico Vichi**

The year is 1982. Audriada Mikolos is twenty-four years old when she arrives in New York City with the dream of becoming a Radio City Music Hall Rockette. A native of Greece, she uses what little English she knows to convince an old Italian man to let her move in to his three-room apartment. Using what little English *he* knows, he convinces her to audition for the New York City Ballet instead.

What follows is the story of Audra and Pietro. Set in Little Italy back in the days before it was swallowed by Chinatown—the days before the tourists and the "bridge-and-tunnel" bars—it chronicles the maturation of their friendship as they seek to learn each other's language and come to terms with each other's culture.

It takes her several tries, but Audra does eventually make the ballet, and what happens to her on opening night changes Pietro's life forever, in ways both subtle and profound. A poignant tale of two very different people who transcend the limits they've placed on themselves, *Terpsichore's Muse* will resonate with anyone who has ever been believed in.

Nico Vichi is the co-author of *Dancing in the Dark: One Man's Year in the Russian Ballet* (Amber Press, 2001). He holds a B.F.A. in modern dance from New York University. A graduate of Columbia University's M.F.A program in Creative Writing, Vichi is making his first foray into fiction. For more information please visit his Web site: www.nicovichi.com.

> "*Terpsichore's Muse* is at once an ode to the redemptive power of art and a paean to the power of human friendship. Vichi treads on sacred ground—lightly, but with solid footing."—*Library Journal*
>
> "A triple pirouette of a book."—*Booklist*

September 15, 2002 • Fiction
Hardcover • 266 Pages • $26.00 • ISBN: 0-1234-5678-9

Stillwater Press

712 Pond Street, Cambridge, Massachusetts 02142

(617) 555-1234 ph. / (617) 555-5678 fx.

www.stillwaterpress.com

Contact: Calla McKittrick, Director of Publicity

(617) 555-1234 / calla.mckittrick@stillwaterpress.com

Announcing the Arrival of a New Parenting Book . . .

Sleeping Through the Night

by Haywood Adams Barr, M.D.

with Karen Broadside

"Few pediatricians understand children as Haywood Adams Barr does."

—John S. Peters, former U.S. Surgeon General

Sleepless nights. It's an ever-present issue for moms and dads. Now, one of America's most trusted pediatricians, Dr. Haywood Adams Barr, offers support with an indispensable guide that leads parents step-by-step through this struggle, providing a window into their infant, toddler, or young child's behavior—one that will enable them to come up with solutions that are right for their particular family.

Covering everything moms and dads need to know to help their young one get a good night's rest, Sleeping Through the Night explains how to help a baby soothe itself back to sleep, how to safeguard against SIDS, how to wean a child from the "family bed," and what to do about sleepwalking and nightmares.

Sleeping Through the Night also tackles a common but little acknowl-edged condition— infant insomnia—about which Dr. Adams Barr is considered to be the country's foremost expert. An "I. I." baby is one who gets fewer than ten hours of sleep a day and whose primary sleeping hours are from 2:00 A.M. to noon. Dr. Adams Barr explains what causes this irregularity and what can be done to fix it.

Haywood Adams Barr, M.D. has been a pediatrician in private practice for more than twenty-five years. The father of four, he lives in Tampa, Florida. He'll launch his book with an appearance on *Good Morning America* on February 22nd, followed by a twenty-market TV satellite tour.

March 1, 2002 • Parenting • Paperback Original
186 Pages • $11.95 • ISBN: 0-1234-5678-9

PRESS RELEASES (PAPERBACK REPRINTS)
Recommended Length: 1–2 Pages

Stillwater Press

712 Pond Street, Cambridge, Massachusetts 02142

(617) 555-1234 ph. / (617) 555-5678 fx.

www.stillwaterpress.com

Contact: Calla McKittrick, Director of Publicity

(617) 555-1234 / calla.mckittrick@stillwaterpress.com

Now Available in a New Paperback Edition . . .

A Cornucopia of Corn

100 *Classic Recipes—From Chowder to the Cob*
By James P. Parker and Sharon Simpson

First published in 1982, *A Cornucopia of Corn* was hailed by the *New York Times* as "the essential guide to this most American of vegetables." Now, Stillwater Press is proud to present a new paperback edition, complete with a dozen new recipes—everything from Cornflake Casserole and Caramel Corn, to Spicy Corn Salsa and Crunchy Corn Fritters.

These new concoctions take their place alongside such classics as Ma Olsson's Cornbread and Pickled Corn, the dish that won the *Ladies' Home Journal* "Gold Star" award in 1952. From "A-maize-ing Popcorn" to "Top-Notch Tortillas," each recipe contains a sidebar of helpful hints to save you preparation time and money.

Of course, no book on corn would be complete without directions for the perfect chowder. *A Cornucopia of Corn*'s chowder contains russet potatoes and celery, with just a dash of freshly ground pepper. There's even a recipe for the perfect ear of corn and the salt-butter sauce to pour upon it.

With a new introduction by Martha Egret, Director of the Native American Food Museum, *A Cornucopia of Corn* is the perfect addition to any cookbook shelf.

James P. Parker, author of *The Great American Bean Book*—winner of the 1994 James Beard Award—owns and runs Magellan's, a five-star eatery in southwest Oklahoma. **Sharon Simpson** is Chief Food Critic for the *Dallas Morning News* and co-author of *Sugar in the Morning: 100 Recipes to Make Your Breakfast Sweet*.

November 1, 2002 • Cooking • 6 x 5 Paperback
214 Pages • 52 Line Drawings • $18.00
ISBN: 0-1234-5678-9

Stillwater Press

712 Pond Street, Cambridge, Massachusetts 02142

(617) 555-1234 ph. / (617) 555-5678 fx.

www.stillwaterpress.com

Contact: Calla McKittrick, Director of Publicity

(617) 555-1234 / calla.mckittrick@stillwaterpress.com

Now Available in Paperback . . .

Career Kamikazes
Self-Sabotage in the Workplace
Alexander Lambert, Walter Locke,
Erin Masters, and David Pearlstein

A *Business Week* and *Wall Street Journal* Bestseller

When *Career Kamikazes* first came off press last year, it generated a firestorm of controversy. *Fortune* magazine called the authors "rabble rousers." One critic hailed it as "a brilliant piece of total bunk." Meanwhile, Amazon.com's Jeff Bezos personally recommended it in a letter that he posted on his site, and a team of J. P. Morgan private bankers put it on a summer reading list for their millionaire clients.

Soon, the book started popping onto bestseller lists. In the end, it totaled seven months on the *Business Week* list, three consecutive months on the *New York Times* business bestseller list, and an appearance on the *Wall Street Journal*'s business list. Amazon.com selected it as one of the top ten business books of 2001, and it made *USA Today*'s "Money" section list of best-selling business books of the year.

So what's all the fuss? *Career Kamikazes* is the first book to thoroughly examine self-sabotage in the workplace—the act of hurting your own career through tantrums, Napoleonic complexes, and other prima donna behavior. And it names names, analyzing executives at some of the country's foremost corporations and showing how their boorish behavior has undermined their ability to lead (and led to their eventual demise). What's more, it lists ten CEOs whose days are numbered. Since the book's original publication, two of them have indeed been fired, and a new afterword by the authors puts their departures in perspective, proving that *Career Kamikazes* do, eventually, get what they subconsciously desire.

About the Authors

Alexander Lambert, Walter Locke, Erin Masters, and **David Pearlstein** are co-owners of the career consulting firm Lambert, Locke, Masters, and Pearlstein, Inc., whose clients include the CEOs of numerous Fortune 500 companies. Based in Manhattan, the company was founded in 1987 and has been profiled in such publications as *Fast Company*, *Business Week*, and *Business 2.0*. Lambert is a graduate of Harvard Business School and teaches at New York University. Locke attended the Wharton School of Business and is a frequent contributor to *Across the Board* and *Chief Executive* magazine. Masters has a Ph.D. in Personnel Psychology from the University of Michigan and specializes in corporate culture. Pearlstein completed his studies at Princeton University and served as CEO of Motorola for seven years before joining the firm in 1998. Visit their Web site at www.LLMPinc.com.

**February 1, 2002 • Business • Paperback • 190 Pages
$14.00 • ISBN: 0-1234-5678-9**

Stillwater Press
712 Pond Street, Cambridge, Massachusetts 02142
(617) 555-1234 ph. / (617) 555-5678 fx.
www.stillwaterpress.com

Contact: Calla McKittrick, Director of Publicity
(617) 555-1234 / calla.mckittrick@stillwaterpress.com

Just in Time for Spring Break

New Edition Offers Updated Information
on Where to Stay and What to Do in Mexico

Cancun. Cozumel. Cabo San Lucas. These are just some of the wonderful cities in Mexico, and they, along with dozens of others, are the subject of *The Grotto Guide to Mexico*, now available in a new edition that contains updated information on the country's best hotels, restaurants, day spots, and nightlife.

Whether you enjoy snorkeling, beachcombing, jet-skiing and parasailing, or shopping, sightseeing, and eating native cuisine, *The Grotto Guide* will serve as your personal concierge, pointing out famous and little-known haunts including:

- the ancient Mayan ruins of Chichen Itza and Tulum
- the underground rivers of Parque Xcaret
- the lagoons and natural wells of Xel-Ha
- the galleries and boutiques at Plaza Caracol
- the black-coral factories on Isla Mujeres
- the restaurant El Pescador where the fish is cooked in banana leaves
- the bar Señor Frogs with its dueling tequila fountains

Compiled by the editors of *Grotto*, a hip young magazine based in Mexico City with offices throughout the Yucatan Peninsula, *The Grotto Guide* offers insider advice from people who work—and play—there. With maps, bus schedules, and everything you'll need to navigate the country—including a handy list of Spanish phrases to get you around—*The Grotto Guide to Mexico* will help you make the most of your vacation.

March 15, 2003 • Travel • Paperback • 228 Pages • $15.95
ISBN: 0-1234-5678-9

Q & As
Recommended Length: 3–5 Pages

An Interview with the Novelist Samuel Dash
Author of *Slantwalk*

Is it true that "Slantwalk" is the nickname for a sidewalk that ran across your college campus?
Man, you guys do your homework. Yeah, it's true. I went to Miami University undergrad—the one in Ohio, not the Florida one. They had this red brick sidewalk that cut through the main quad, and it kind of connected the bars and the dorms. It made it much easier to make it home drunk. Somehow I don't think that's what they intended. Anyway, in the book, it was kind of a metaphor for something you have to follow in order to find yourself. But it wasn't a normal path, you see. It was kind of one-off, like my character. And of course, in the book, the path was in Boston.

Your character is Tommy Rad, a Southie kid who goes to Harvard. Sounds kind of like *Good Will Hunting*, if you don't mind my saying so.
Well, of course I get that a lot. But Radzinski isn't a genius. In fact, he's kind of stupid, especially in math. He gets in to Harvard because his pop has pull with the Dean of Students. Besides, I wrote this book eleven years ago—before that movie even went into production. I did like the flick though. Maybe Damon will play Tommy Rad if we sell the movie rights.

Tell me about your writing process.
It goes kind of like this: Wake up around eleven or so—noon if it's the weekend. Put on my bathrobe and sit down at the computer.

See if the spirit moves me. If it does, I write all day. If it don't, I go get a bagel.

Do you tinker a lot as you're writing, or do you just try to get words on the page and then go back and fix them later?
Depends. Usually the first one. You wouldn't think it by looking at me, but I'm kind of a perfectionist. It's hard for me to move on when I know the words aren't right.

The late Andre Dubus once said that short stories are closer to poems than to novels. You've dabbled in all three genres. Do you think that's true?
I would never disagree with a damn thing that man said. What a friggin' genius. Have you ever read "A Father's Story?" God, that thing will kill you. And I'm not even a dad. I even like his essays. That *Broken Vessels* book with the one about the lambs. I'm not very religious, but damn that essay moved me. Seriously though, he's right about that. Stories and poems are cousins. Novels are related, but not by blood.

Back to your book for a minute. How long did it take you to write *Slantwalk*, and why did it take so long to get it published?
Only a year and a half. I know, I know—you're supposed to labor over it. Well, it was my first book, and I didn't know that yet. As for why it took so long to get published, god, I dunno. I mean, after the first round of rejections—and keep in mind I didn't have an agent then— I let it sit in my desk drawer for six or seven years. Then Amanda Bourbon—that's my agent; great name, eh?—then Amanda found out about it from my girlfriend, and made me dig it out and give it to her. And hey, she liked it. I had to spend time fixing it up. I'd matured a lot as a writer by then. The dialogue was shit and the pacing was off. But the characters and the plot are the same. Once it was tight she started to shop it. And the rest is history, as they say.

In *Slantwalk*, Tommy Rad does a lot of drugs. Care to comment on that?

Well . . . what can I say? It's set in the '80s. All Southie kids smoked pot back then. Maybe they still do. As for the other stuff, I can't recommend it. I mean, I'm not going to say that I sit around at parties drinking tea. But I'm not the one in the bathroom doing the line of coke either, you know?

Tommy's girlfriend, Jezebel, is one of my all-time favorite female characters. Did you base her on someone? Your girlfriend, perhaps?

No, she's a composite. I like to think of her as a little Janis Joplin with maybe a little Debbie Harry thrown in. She's ballsy like my girlfriend, but my gal is all straight-laced. She's Park Ave. and I'm East Village. Anyway, Jezebel is very much the driving force behind Tommy. Everything he accomplishes he does because of her.

Do you think that's true of most relationships?

I think in most relationships one person has to be the pusher and the other has to be the pushee. If they're both the pusher, they end up beating the hell out of each other. Maybe literally. If they're both the pushee, well, they starve to death. But I don't think men are one way and women are the other. It can vary. Why all of a sudden am I thinking of Yoko?

Because she was the ultimate pusher?

Yeah, that's it. Right.

Toward the end of *Slantwalk*, Tommy learns that he's going to be a dad. But we see no sign that he'll straighten out. Do you think he does?

I tried to hint at that. I think if you read it again, you'll see it. He does begin to get his shit together. The doing laundry before he runs out of clothes. The remembering to buy toilet paper before he's like, sitting there, realizing he's out. That sort of thing. It's subtle, but it's there. I guess I do have faith in him—faith in all of us, really, that when we have to give up and grow up, we somehow manage to do it.

For further information or to schedule an interview with Samuel Dash,
please contact:
Calla McKittrick, Director of Publicity
(617) 555-1234 / calla.mckittrick@stillwaterpress.com

―――――――――

A Talk with the Essayist Rory Campbell
Author of *Minute Particulars*

What's the significance of the title of your book?
I borrowed it from William Blake: "Seek poetry in minute particulars." Each essay takes an object as its subject and mines it until something is revealed—something human, or important, or profound. Something that's poetic. At least, that's the idea.

Tell us how you chose the objects.
Lord, I wish I knew. They were like stray cats that came and stayed awhile. And pretty soon, I couldn't remember which cat I had asked to be there, and which cat had simply made itself at home. The bowl of apples came from a Cezanne painting, I suppose. I couldn't say which one, and in my mind they were shinier than any that he painted. I almost see it as a bowl of little moons.

What about the Loosestrife? What made you think of that?
Well, it's outside my window, I guess. My writing room overlooks

a brook, and each July it's strangled by the stuff. It really is a nasty weed, but beautiful to look at. That's what I was like in my twenties—mean and greedy but pleasing to the eye. And that's what looking at the Loosestrife taught me. That was the poem it offered.

My favorite essay is the one about the sow. You live in Connecticut—where'd you find a pig?
My next door neighbor has one. Believe it or not, they make very good pets. Smart as a dog, and just as loyal. I spent three days in my neighbor's yard just looking at that sow, watching her just sun herself, eating all that she was offered. There's much that we can learn from that. In my thirties and forties I worked very hard. I put my children first. I teetered on exhaustion and whole years glided by. I denied myself the things I wanted—a job that would take me away from home; some calories; a lover.

The fifth essay is about bulimia, is it not?
It is, I suppose, though not directly. It's about a doll named Ethel. She has no hair and her fingers are rough and her teeth have disintegrated. Infer from it what you will. I did, of course, battle the disease. But the essay is more about what we do to keep ourselves presentable—the lengths to which we'll go to make it look like all is well.

You dedicate the book to Jonah. Jonah is . . . ?
My cat. He ignored me while I wrote this book, but his presence was a comfort. There's a great history of authors and cats. Also authors and painters.

You mention artists throughout your book—Modigliani several times.
Oh yes, I like his work. Very, very much. His portraits are my favorite. The Jean Cocteau—he loathed the man, but gave him the

neck of a swan. And *Girl with Braids*—the longest face and emptiest of eyes. And the one of his fiancée. She was pregnant with his second child when he died. She marched to the roof of her father's house and threw herself right off it. Almost nine months pregnant. My God, can you imagine?

Is this book like your others?
It feels different to me, actually. More accessible. More open. *Merganser* was ethereal. The next one was grounded, but lacked a certain "heart." This one is the best I've done as far as I'm concerned. But, of course, there haven't been reviews yet.

Do you read the reviews your books receive?
I most certainly do. Every word. Anyone who says she doesn't is a liar.

What do you think when you get a good review?
I think the reviewer is a genius, of course.

And if it's bad?
An idiot. A total fool. A dolt.

You delivered a lecture at Yale last year—sort of a "State of the Essay." You've always been a fan of the form, have you not?
I have been. And that scares me. I do not think that Americans know how to write an essay. The French can do it. Even the Brits. But we feel the need to embellish. At its core, the essay should be nothing more than a means to convey and defend a concept. It should not be used to ruminate; simply to inform. I say this as a hypocrite.

Tell me about the last essay, "Nautilus."
It refers to the Chambered Nautilus, of course. Not the gym

equipment. I am fascinated by this shell—all those tiny limestone walls. We are taught early on that we must learn to trust—our parents, our siblings; eventually, our mate. And she—it is almost certainly a she—says "No, I will build these, I must wall you off," and goes about her business, and spirals up, not down. Plus she has those pearl-white walls no one can take a crayon to.

But surely you don't regret having children?
Not at all. But many women do. Look at a turtle long enough—you'll see it.

To schedule an interview with Rory Campbell, please contact:
Calla McKittrick, Director of Publicity
(617) 555-1234 / calla.mckittrick@stillwaterpress.com

A Conversation with Kimberly Hanson and Janet Land
Authors of
The Roaring Twenties: Women, Work, and a Decade Wasted

You acknowledge that a woman's twenties can be an exciting time for her, careerwise—first real job, rapid advancement, major spike in pay. How, then, can you call it a "wasted" decade?
KH: I think most women don't realize, at the time, that the decade is being wasted. Many women in their twenties find joy in their job—in the work itself, in their co-workers, in their ability to support themselves financially. The problem is they wake up one day, and realize they've sacrificed everything—time with family, time with friends, the time it takes to find a mate and nurture that relationship—and that what they've gained—an exciting career—somehow leaves them empty.

Don't you worry that people will see your message as anti-feminist?
JL: Not at all. Feminism is about doing what you want to do. What we're saying is that women today feel like they don't have a choice—not if they really want to get ahead. They think they must throw themselves into work in order to climb the ladder. They think that they must work late hours, and possibly weekends, and certainly nights. We want to empower women to set limits—not *on* themselves but on *how much* of themselves they are willing to give to their jobs.

So you're not saying women shouldn't have careers?
JL: Definitely not. They should—provided that's what they want.

You're both in your early thirties now. What were your twenties like? Do you have these regrets?
KH: I graduated from college in 1993. I did take the summer to travel, then in the fall I got a job in New York at a magazine. I worked tremendous hours—sometimes sixty, sometimes more. Between '93 and '99, I took one vacation—just a week. I did advance quite nicely, making a jump from editorial assistant to associate editor in less than a year, then two years later to editor, then senior editor, then editor-in-chief which is what I am right now. I'm proud of my accomplishments. And I've had a lot of fun along the way. But my grandmother died during this time, and I don't feel I was there for my mom—not as much as I should have been. And I had two good relationships, either of which could have led to marriage, but both of which dissolved because I did not make them enough of a priority. So yes, I have regrets.
JL: After college, I got a job at a major marketing firm. I continued to work full time while I got my MBA. In the span of a decade, I went from entry level to senior director, and shortly after that I was promoted to VP. Unlike Kim, I did not have any serious relationships. I dated a little—whenever there was time. Because my family lived close by, I never felt shortchanged that way. But I did have to give up dancing, which is

something I'd done all my life. Most nights I couldn't make it to the studio before it closed. Or I felt like I couldn't, at any rate.

What do you say when people tell you to suck it up—that that's what it takes to get ahead; that that's the price you pay?
KH: I say, "Maybe, but that's not how it should be." And I remind them that a difference exists between how hard a man has to work to get ahead and how much effort is required of a woman.

What kind of research did you do for this book?
KH: We interviewed more than two hundred women, all of them in their thirties. They varied by race and location, but all were what we'd call "professional," usually in white-collar industries like law or medicine or academia. A lot of them were "corporate"—finance, accounting, that sort of thing.

Why do you call them the "roaring" twenties?
JL: Because they go by like a freight train—big, and fast, and loud, and hectic. And once they're gone, you find yourself staring at a very empty track. That's when the ticking starts.

The biological clock?
KH: Yes, exactly. There have been some books about it. Most of the women chronicled in them were married with no kids. Our data suggests it's worse than that. More than sixty percent of the women we spoke with weren't even married. So tack on another year or two—at least—to find a mate. Clock's getting pretty loud by then if you believe the fertility data.

Why do you think this problem exists? Why does it take most women a decade to realize they've sacrificed too much? Why do they make this sacrifice in the first place?

KH: I think it stems from a desire not to squander the chance that we've been given. We're aware that the opportunity for a meaningful, financially rewarding career did not always exist—that it's something the women who came before us fought for. We feel the need to honor that.

JL: As for why it takes so long, loyalty plays a role. During their twenties, most women work for two different companies, most men for four. Women feel disloyal if they leave work early—or even just on time—to do anything that isn't somehow work-related. Ask them to take a long hard look at how their company takes them for granted, and they start to feel guilty just thinking about it.

So what do we do about all of this. How do we stop the roar?

KH: I think it's different for each of us. I think some of us need to ask for an assistant or an extra head in our department. We need to stop seeing it as a sign of weakness; men demand them all the time. I think some of us need to take our vacations. I think some of us need to take a sabbatical so that we can pursue other passions—writing a book, teaching a course, whatever floats your boat. I think some of us need to "just say no" when we're handed an extra assignment.

JL: And I think companies have to address this. I think every woman in her twenties should be paired with a mentor in her thirties or forties—someone who can guide her, and help her gain perspective.

To arrange an interview with Kimberly Hanson and Janet Land,
please contact:
Calla McKittrick, Director of Publicity
(617) 555-1234 ph / calla.mckittrick@stillwaterpress.com

QUESTION SHEETS
Recommended Length: 1 Page

Questions for Bill Marschal
Author of *Supergeeks: How Net Heads Are Poised to Take Over the World*

Could you define a Supergeek for us? How different are Supergeeks from the guys we saw in *Revenge of the Nerds*? How different is a Supergeek from a Jock?

Is a Supergeek made or born?

You call M.I.T. the "Supergeek Mothership." Aren't you afraid of offending your alma mater? And hey, doesn't that make you a Supergeek?

Are all Supergeeks Net Heads, and are all Net Heads Supergeeks?

You refer to San Jose as "Supergeek Mecca." Is that still true, even after the burst of the Internet bubble?

In Chapter Nine, you refer to the "Übergeek," but never formally name him. Can we assume you mean Bill Gates?

Will WiFi give Supergeeks more power or just make them more mobile?

Explain the iPod—Supergeek toy or too cool for Supergeeks? Or maybe Supergeeks are too cool for it?

You paint Al Gore as a Supergeek wanna-be. Are there other

hangers-on who will never quite make it into the Supergeek stratosphere?

In your last chapter, you look ahead to the 2004 presidential election and hypothesize that the candidate with the best web presence will win. Based on what you've seen so far, who's it going to be?

To schedule an interview with Bill Marschal, please contact:
Calla McKittrick, Director of Publicity
(617) 555-1234 / calla.mckittrick@stillwaterpress.com

Questions for Erin Rodale
Author of *A Rose by Any Other Name*

What first motivated you to learn the art of flower arranging, and how did that lead you to formally study flowers?

What are some examples of how flowers have evolved? How have humans affected the evolution of flowers?

What is the most interesting thing about flowers that most people don't know?

What can we learn from flowers?

What are the medicinal capabilities of flowers? How much research is being done to discover these capabilities?

How has the significance of flowers changed over time? Do flowers maintain the kind of symbolic weight they once had?

In Chapter Eight, you discuss our developing ability to manipulate the characteristics of flowers. Where is the genetic engineering of flowers headed and how do you feel about it?

There's a rose in the title of your book. Is that your favorite flower? Is it possible for a florist to have a favorite, or is that like asking a mother to choose between her children?

The Snapdragon. The Pink Lady's Slipper. The Tiger Lily. Flowers have amazing names. Where do they get them? Who gets the honor of naming them?

What steps would you recommend to people interested in learning more about flowers?

To schedule an interview with Erin Rodale, please contact:
Calla McKittrick, Director of Publicity
(617) 555-1234 / calla.mckittrick@stillwaterpress.com

A Dozen Questions for Sarah Dodson
Author of *A Girl's Best Friend?: The Diamond Throughout History*

How did you personally become interested in diamonds?

How have diamonds influenced the course of human history?

In your book, you talk about the thousands of people who have died over diamonds. Who do you hold responsible for this—the people who own the mines or the consumer who keeps buying their product?

Where did the research for this book take you?

Your chapter "The Diamond and the Diva" looks at everything from Marilyn Monroe's sultry rendition of "Diamonds Are a Girl's Best Friend" to Jennifer Lopez's pink-diamond engagement ring. Tell us about other celebrities that have been associated with diamonds.

When and how did the diamond engagement ring become the norm?

You devote a whole chapter to the Hope diamond. How come?

There has been a lot in the news lately about our newfound ability to engineer these gems in the lab. Do you think these "manufactured" diamonds will ever take hold?

What's your take on the current state of the diamond industry?

What scientific, medical, and technological advances could the diamond make possible?

What lessons can we draw from the history of the diamond?

One last question—what's your favorite cut and color?

To schedule an interview with Sarah Dodson, please contact:
Calla McKittrick, Director of Publicity
(617) 555-1234 / calla.mckittrick@stillwaterpress.com

TALKING POINTS SHEETS
Recommended Length: 1–3 Pages

How to Proofread Like a Pro
Adapted from *To Err Is Human* by Lisa Grupman-Knox

Whether you've written a formal letter or a report, a dissertation or a marketing plan, it's important to proofread what you've crafted. Here are seven tips to get you started:

1. Take advantage of technology by using the spell check (and, if offered, the grammar check) that came with your computer.

2. Give the document a once-over for common mistakes the auto checks may have missed—to/too/two, there/their/ they're, stationary/stationery, complimentary/ complementary, etc.

3. Read the document twice—once for content (is there a place where something doesn't make sense?), and once for all the nuts and bolts (punctuation, spelling, etc.).

4. Guard against inconsistency. Do you refer to a woman as "Ms." in one place and "Miss" in another? Are you doing things "asap" and "ASAP?" Is this "FYI" and "f.y.i.?"

5. Share the material with a friend or colleague. Four eyes are always better than two (unless you're in sixth grade and wearing glasses).

6. Read the piece out loud to discover awkward phrases, omitted words, etc.

7. Put the document aside for a while and look at it again when you're fresh.

What You May Not Know About the College Classroom
Adapted from *Campus* by David J. Kincaid

A third of the students who attend the first day of class are no longer enrolled in the class by the last day.

The average number of students in an undergraduate course is fifty-two. In a graduate course, it's fourteen.

Seventy-eight percent of college professors have had a student throw up in class. Ninety-eight percent have had at least one student show up drunk.

Most students miss at least five classes a semester in a twice-a-week course and two classes a semester in a once-a-week course.

Only twenty-one percent of professors give pop quizzes. One out of every three finals is a take-home.

Eighty-two percent of undergrads call their professor by his or her first name. For grad students, it's ninety-nine percent.

Two out of every ten professors claim to have slept with at least one student. More often than not, these professors are female.

On average, a professor fails four students per semester.

One in every ten students has had some form of intimate sexual contact in a lecture hall—during class—by the time they graduate.

It's estimated that, last year, more than 350,000 U.S. college students attended at least one class high on marijuana. For professors, the number was 17,000.

Most professors have not revised their syllabus in seven years.

Seventy-two percent of students have cheated on a final. Plagiarism rates are at twenty-two percent.

Sixty-three percent of students have lied about their missing homework. The number one excuse: a death in the family.

Forty-six percent of students say they've fallen asleep in class.

The number of hours per week most students watch TV: twenty-one. The number of hours per week most students study: eight.

AUTHOR BIOS
Recommended Length: 1 Page

Joseph Price
Author of *The Hole Story: A Biography of Courtney Love*

Joseph Price is Chief Music Critic at the *Los Angeles Times*. A graduate of Boston's prestigious Berklee College of Music where he majored in guitar, Mr. Price has toured the United States and Europe with his band Whippersnapper, whose 1994 album, *Steady Now*, sold over three-million copies.

Mr. Price's previous books include *Pure Nirvana: The Kurt Cobain Story*, *Punk: The Story of a Musical Era*, and *Grunge: The History of Music's Future*, winner of the 2000 ASCAP Deems Taylor Award, the highest honor for a work of music criticism.

A former Contributing Editor at *Rolling Stone*, Mr. Price's work has appeared in *Spin*, *Blender*, *The New Yorker*, *Vanity Fair*, and numerous other music and culture magazines. His 2001 profile of No Doubt's Gwen Steffani, which appeared in *Mojo*, garnered him appearances on E! and MTV.

In 2002, Mr. Price took a six-month sabbatical to study Britain's underground music scene. His research was featured in the BBC documentary "Way Down Deep."

Mr. Price was selected to write the first entry for "Punk Music" in the *Encyclopedia Britannica* and has appeared on such National Public Radio programs as *All Things Considered*, *Morning Edition*, *Talk of the Nation*, and *The Connection*. Born in New York City in 1968, he currently lives in Los Angeles, California.

Evan Zupanski

Named in a 2001 *Financial Times* Group survey as one of the "top 50 business thinkers in the world," Evan Zupanski is the author of *Risky Business: High Stakes Investing in Low Economic Times.* The CFO of Adwater, Zupanski, & Associates, one of the country's most elite investment firms, he is a noted industry speaker, having keynoted for such organizations as Citibank, Citizen's Bank, Fleet Bank, and American Express. He received the National Investment Council's 1999 Orberger-Stafford Award for his contribution to the world of personal finance, and now sits on the organization's board of directors.

Zupanski has written extensively for such publications as *Forbes, Fortune, CFO* magazine, and the *Harvard Business Review.* His professional work has been covered by the *Economist, Inc.* magazine, the *New York Times,* and the *Wall Street Journal,* which recently hailed him as "one of money's most intriguing minds." He is a frequent guest on National Public Radio's *Sound Money,* and appears regularly on CNBC's *Power Lunch.* In 2002 he appeared in the PBS documentary "Corporate America." Zupanski's previous book, *The Role of Money in the Modern World,* spent eight weeks on the *Wall Street Journal*'s bestseller list and was translated into seven languages.

Mr. Zupanski is a graduate of Yale University and has an MBA from Harvard Business School. He is an adjunct professor at Northwestern University, where his class on mutual funds is one of their most requested graduate courses. Prior to founding Adwater, Zupanski, & Associates, Zupanski was employed by the Midwest Economic Advisory Group. He lives in Chicago, Illinois.

About the Authors of *A Minor Year*

Phil *Aldenbacher*

A Boston Red Sox fan since birth and the recipient of the Columbia School of Journalism's 2001 Sportswriter of the Year Award, Phil Aldenbacher is a sports columnist for the *Boston Globe*. Previously, he was a staff writer at the *Providence Journal* where his five-part series on the Triple-A Pawtucket Red Sox earned him a Pulitzer Prize nomination. Aldenbacher has covered Minor League baseball for ESPN.com, ESPN magazine, and *Sports Illustrated*. His first job out of college was crunching stats for MinorLeagueBaseball.com. Aldenbacher appears regularly on New England Cable News to talk about the region's minor league teams. He lives in Waltham, Massachusetts.

Ethan *Gerstner*

A graduate of Northeastern University and a former shortstop for the Portland Sea Dogs, Ethan Gerstner retired from baseball in 1995 after a career-ending injury to his knee. Throughout his time in the minors, he kept the journal that went on to serve as the basis for this book. Gerstner now resides in Tucson, Arizona, where he manages the Triple-A Tucson Sidewinders. In 2002, he was voted Minor League Coach of the Year by *USA Today's Baseball Weekly*, making him the first former player to receive such an honor.

Justin *O'Claray*

A former college baseball coach, Justin O'Claray has served as a scout for the New York Yankees since 2001 and is credited with finding some of their most promising minor league prospects. O'Claray is a frequent guest on *Sporting News* Radio and his oldest son, Michael O'Claray, played for the Lowell Spinners last summer.

QUIZZES
Recommended Length: 1–2 Pages

How Much Do You Know About Seashells?
Take this true/false quiz and find out . . .

1. There are five different classes of seashells.
2. The conch shell is an example of a bivalve.
3. Tooth shells resemble elephant tusks rather than human teeth.
4. The octopus and the squid are categorized as having shells.
5. The scallop is an example of a univalve.
6. Chitons are shells with many plates.
7. Cowrie shells were once used as money.
8. Coral is a type of shell.
9. The animal that creates the shell is called the mollusk.
10. The "rubber band" that holds together a clamshell is called the abductor muscle.
11. The limpet is a univalve that closely resembles a little volcano.
12. Catspaws are normally orange and white.
13. Bleeding teeth are usually found attached to rocks.
14. Hermit crabs often take over abandoned seashells.
15. The "trap door" of a univalve that protects it from intruders is called the operculum.
16. The best way to find a sand dollar is to start digging.
17. December through April is the best time to find seashells in Florida.
18. Baby oil is a harmful way to shine up a seashell.
19. Burying, freezing, boiling, bleaching, and microwaving are common methods of cleaning shells.

20. The periostracum is the flaky leathery covering on top of most seashells.
21. It's best to go shelling and beachcombing around high tide.
22. The better the weather, the better the shelling.
23. Some beaches don't allow you to remove shells that still have the animal inside them.
24. There are over 60,000 species of shells.
25. There's a network of shell clubs throughout the U.S., with members who meet to compare their finds.

Answer Key:

1.T	2. F	3.T	4.T	5. F	6.T	7.T	8. F
9.T	10.T	11.T	12.T	13.T	14.T	15.T	16.T
17.T	18. F	19.T	20.T	21. F	22. F	23.T	24.T
25.T							

Adapted from *Beachcombing: A Beginner's Guide* by Jennifer Priest.

How Good of an Interviewer Are You?
Take this multiple choice quiz and find out . . .

1. Interviewees list their least favorite interview question as
   a. So, tell me about yourself.
   b. Why do you want to work for our company?
   c. What kind of supervisor do you like?
   d. Why did you leave your previous job?/Why are you looking to leave your current job?

2. When candidates appears nervous, the best way to make them feel at ease is to
  a. Offer them tea or coffee.
  b. Tell them you were impressed with their resume.
  c. Acknowledge verbally that interviews can be nerve-wracking.
  d. Excuse yourself for a moment so that they can collect themselves.

3. When candidates appears nervous, you should take it as a sign that
  a. They really want the job.
  b. They really need the job.
  c. They're probably too high-strung to do the job effectively.
  d. a or b.

4. When candidates don't bring an extra copy of their resume, you should infer that
  a. They know it's not necessary, in this age of email and fax.
  b. They're forgetful.
  c. They have no knowledge of standard interview procedure, which is a minimum requirement.
  d. They feel under- or over-qualified for the job.

5. When interviewees don't send a thank-you notes, it means
  a. They're not interested in the job.
  b. They're not familiar with basic protocol for interview follow-up.
  c. They have poor manners.
  d. All of the above.

6. A candidate looks great on paper and interviews well. But something doesn't feel right. You should
  a. Go with your gut and hire someone else.

b. Have him in for a second interview.

c. Ask a colleague or supervisor to interview him.

d. Hire him anyway.

7. You catch a typo in an applicant's resume. You should
    a. Invite him in for an interview anyway, assuming he is qualified.
    b. Put the resume at the bottom of the pile.
    c. Throw the resume out.
    d. Alert him that there's a typo and see how he responds.

8. You ask for a reference and the candidate says he can't supply one because he doesn't want his current employer to know he's looking. You should infer that
    a. He has something to hide.
    b. He's telling the truth.
    c. he must not want the job.
    d. Any of the above.

9. It's appropriate for an interviewee to ask about salary, vacation time, bonuses, etc.
    a. During the first interview.
    b. During the second interview.
    c. When the offer is made.
    d. Never.

10. All offers should be made
    a. Over the phone.
    b. Face-to-face.
    c. In writing.
    d. a and c.

Answers: 1. A, 2. B, 3. D, 4. C, 5. B, 6. A, 7. C, 8. A, 9. C, 10. D

Scoring: 8–10 Correct = You're a great interviewer!

Fewer than 8 Correct = Read *Interviewing: Part Art, Part Science* by Bridget Hawkins

---

How Much Do You Know About the Romance Novels of Mary Larkman?

Match Her Characters with Their Books

1. ___ Genevieve DeSoto	A. *Winter on the Vineyard*
2. ___ Caroline Donovan	B. *In a Bad Way*
3. ___ Cecilia Rhodes	C. *Ivory*
4. ___ Alexis Lambert	D. *Madrid*
5. ___ Carrie August	E. *When I Say the Word*
6. ___ Julia Harman	F. *Summer in the Hamptons*
7. ___ Helena Finch	G. *Warblers*
8. ___ Anna Landon	H. *White Sangria*
9. ___ Sidney Tate	I. *What the Water Wrought*
10. ___ Elena Castillo	J. *Rouge*
11. ___ Iliana Rimbaldi	K. *The Least Bittern*
12. ___ Delia Bartlett	L. *Bowerbird*
13. ___ Sapna Ash	M. *Feverfew*
14. ___ Charlotte Russell	N. *All Dressed Up*
15. ___ Alida Thompson	O. *Tonic*

Answers:

1. H 2. A 3. N 4. O 5. M 6. I 7. G 8. K 9. F 10. D 11. J 12. L 13. C 14. E 15. B

QUOTE SHEETS
Recommended Length: 1–3 Pages

Advance Praise for Madeleine Santiago's
The First Environment

"Santiago offers the commonest of stories—how she got pregnant, gave birth, and fed her baby—in a most uncommon way. A cross between the quirkily thorough detail of Natalie Angier's science writing and the passionate environmental advocacy of Rachel Carson. . . . Parents to be or anyone concerned with environmental pollution will want to read and discuss this—and act."

—*Publishers Weekly*

"A fabulous book that imparts much more than what is offered in standard pregnancy tomes."

—*Booklist*, STARRED review

"[Santiago] issues a wake-up call in the tradition of Rachel Carson . . . excellent . . . highly recommended."

—*Library Journal*, STARRED review

"A terrifying tale of pregnancy and birth that sounds the alarm about the growing dangers of environmental toxins to parents and their babies. . . . A convincing case that the increasing numbers of babies born with barriers to optimal development are a consequence of environmental insults. Should send parents and would-be parents to the barricades. . . . Mov[es] gracefully between hard science and tender personal anecdotes."

—*Kirkus Reviews*

Praise for *The Self-Esteem Hoax*
By Karen Wolcott, Ph.D.

"Wolcott offers a scathing indictment of the self-esteem movement and its practitioners. . . . Her book provides damning evidence that we have placed undue significance on the concept of self-esteem. . . . This is a book worth reading."

—*American School Board Journal*

"Exposes the state of American education today . . . Dr. Wolcott does an excellent job of identifying many of the current ills afflicting education . . . along with many of the less attractive qualities of the current crop of neglected young."

—*East Bay Express*

"A scorching new book."

—*Baltimore Sun*

"A fascinating and provocative discussion of the impact of the 'self-esteem movement' on American education . . . important."

—*Choice*

"In a country where every other auto bumper bears a sticker proclaiming that the driver's child is an 'honor student,' this attack on the 'empty and very dangerous' concept of self-esteem couldn't be more timely."

—*Publishers Weekly*

"[A] passionately argued and fluidly written attack on contemporary education philosophy and practice . . . provocative."

—*Library Journal*

"The author's style is refreshing; content is informative. Dr. Wolcottt presents a realistic view of why education in America is the way it is."

—*Dallas Morning News*

"Unquestionably, all educators will benefit from Wolcott's reminder that simplifying curricula in order to make kids feel good about themselves cheats them of the opportunity to discover what they can do."

—*Tampa Tribune*

"A scathing polemical survey of where American education stands today on the question of which values are central to the education of children . . . Wolcott documents with great thoroughness and sharp criticism."

—*Los Angeles Times*

"*The Self-Esteem Hoax* will confirm the fears of many and outrage the rest."

—*Todd Mundt Show* (National Public Radio)

Praise for Edward Warchaizer's *The Science of Math*

"*The Science of Math* succeeds in opening our minds to unfamiliar ways of seeing and understanding."

—*Wall Street Journal*

"Warchaizer combines a deep understanding of math with an engaging literary style."

—*Washington Post Book World*

"As entertaining as it is enlightening."

—*Scientific American*

"A mind-opening volume in the best sense of that term . . . a worthy successor to Warchaizer's *The Mathematics of Being.*"

—Boston Herald

"Warchaizer helps us understand the immensely complicated picture that modern physics gives of our world . . . accessible and easy to digest . . . A fascinating introduction to the various mathematical spaces we inhabit."

—Nature

"*The Science of Math* communicates fundamental concepts of modern mathematics and physics to the general reader most effectively."

—New Scientist

"This should be a hit with the literate elite who also appreciate math and science."

—Publishers Weekly

"Help[s] readers understand some of today's most revolutionary ideas in math and physics."

—Science News

"Warchaizer's book presents math's past and its future, while shedding bright light on its present."

—Booklist (American Library Association)

"Breezy and informal . . . knowledgeable readers will have fun."

—Key Reporter (Phi Beta Kappa)

"Warchaizer very clearly explains some of the most complex concepts and theories from mathematics and physics."

—*Roanoke Times*

"A magnificent investigation."

—*Physical Sciences Digest*

"The discussion of mathematical concepts is always clear and accessible . . . This book is bound to be embraced by number fans everywhere."

—Choice

"No matter how much math you've studied, you will learn something new from this book."

—*Science Books & Films*
(American Association for the Advancement of Science)

"A grand tour of geometry."

—*MAA Online* (Mathematical Association of America)

"A fabulous read . . . will make math geeks salivate."

—*Slashdot.com*

TOUR SCHEDULES
Recommended Length: 1–2 Pages

The *No Man Is an Island* Ten-City Tour

New York
The Explorers Club, 9/22, 6:30 P.M. reception, 7:00 P.M. event, seats 105, books sold by Borders

Boston
Globe Corner Bookstore, 9/23, 6:00 P.M. at the First Parish Church, seats 500–600

Chicago
Union League Club, 9/25, 11:30 A.M. meet & greet, noon event, seats 450, books sold by The Bookstall

Washington, D.C.
National Geographic Society, 9/26, 7:30 P.M., seats 385

Seattle
REI Headquarters, 9/29, noon, private talk to their 600 staff members
University Bookstore, 9/29, 7:00 P.M., in Kane Hall, seats 800

Portland
Powell's Books, 9/30, 7:30 P.M. at their main store, seats 300

San Francisco
Commonwealth Club, 10/1, 5:15 P.M. reception, 6:00 P.M. event, seats 250, books sold by Stacey's

Los Angeles
media only, 10/2

Denver
Denver Museum of Nature and Science, 10/3, 1:00 P.M., in their Imax Theater, seats 400, books sold by museum gift shop

Colorado Mountain Club, 10/3, 7:30 P.M., in their American Mountaineering Center Auditorium, seats 350, books sold by Tattered Cover

Minneapolis / St. Paul
Mall of America, 10/5, giant homecoming event in Sears court, 2:00 P.M., books sold by Barnes & Noble

Ruminator Books, 10/6, 7:30 P.M., in Alexander Hill Ballroom at Macalester College

---

The *How to Woo a Hummingbird* Tour

Washington, D.C.
May 23rd
(media only)

Denver, Colorado
June 2nd
Tattered Cover Book Store (at LoDo store as part of Rocky Mountain Land Series), 7:30 P.M.

Santa Fe, New Mexico
June 3rd
Garcia Street Books, 5:30 P.M.

Albuquerque, New Mexico
June 5th
New Mexico Museum of Natural History and Science,
7:00 P.M.

Phoenix, Arizona
June 9th
Changing Hands Book Store (Tempe), 7:00 P.M.

Tucson, Arizona
June 10th
University of Arizona Bookstore, 11:30 A.M.

Seattle, Washington
June 15th
Elliott Bay Book Company, 2:00 P.M.

Portland, Oregon
June 16th
Powell's Books (at Hawthorne store), 7:30 P.M.

San Francisco, California
June 17th
Rakestraw Books, (Danville), 1:00 P.M.
June 18th
Book Passage (Corte Madera), 1:00 P.M.
Barnes & Noble (Berkeley), 7:30 P.M.

Los Angeles, California
June 19th
Borders (Rolling Hills), 7:30 P.M.

Here are sample author tour itineraries:

The Myth of Childhood
Tour Itinerary for Drs. P. K. Walters and Paul Hancock

Emergency Numbers for Aria Johansen (Publicist)
    Work: (212) 555-1234
    Cell: (917) 555-1234
    Home: (212) 555-5678

Please see separate travel itinerary for flight information.

Washington, D.C.

Author escort is Craig Montgomery: 202-555-1234 ph. (202-555-1234 cell)

10/10 8:00 A.M.
Craig picks up Dr. Hancock at his home and drives him to the Willard Hotel: 1401 Pennsylvania Ave NW, Washington, D.C. (202-555-1234).

10/10 8:30 A.M.
Dr. Walters and Aria meet Dr. Hancock and Craig in the lobby of the Willard and proceed to the Voice of America studio.

10/10 9:00-9:30 A.M.

In-studio interview, Voice of America radio, "Book World" show: 330 Independence Ave. SW, Rm. 3440, Washington D.C. (use back entrance on C street between 3rd and 4th; host will meet us at entrance). Contact is Nancy Beardsley (host): 202-555-1234.

10/10 10:00 A.M.

Phone interview, Time.com, Dr. Walters only, with publishing reporter Andrea Sachs (212-555-1234) for her "Galley Girl" column. Sachs to initiate by calling hotel room.

10/10 10:30 A.M.–1:00 P.M.

In-studio interviews (TV Satellite Tour to 10 markets; arranged by Newman Communications), arrive 10:10 to get set up. Address: Reuters studios, 1333 H Street NW, Suite 500, Washington D.C., corner of H and 14th Streets. Reuters contact: Pam Diggins (202-555-1234). Newman contact: David Ratner (617-555-1234).

10/10 1:30–1:45 P.M.

Phone pre-interview to go over questions for Today Show appearance. Contact: Patricia Luchsinger (212-555-1234). Luchsinger to initiate by calling hotel room of Dr. Walters.

10/10 2:00–2:15 P.M.

Phone interview (taped; Dr. Walters only) for Newsweek on Air. Contact: David Alpern (212-555-1234). Alpern to initiate by calling hotel room.

Late lunch in car on way to interview.

10/10 3:00-4:00 or 4:30 P.M.

In-studio interview (taped), Parent's Perspective radio show. Address: Avalon Sound Studio, 4848 Battery Lane, Suite B, Bethesda, MD.

Contacts: Linda Perlis and Sandra Burt (hosts): 301-555-1234 (office); 301-555-1234 (studio).

10/10, 6–7:30 P.M.

Talk at the Library of Congress (see separate itinerary; arrive no later than 5:30 P.M.; you'll have time to freshen up in the greenroom), followed by private dinner. Address: Jefferson Building, Coolidge Auditorium, 10 First Street SE, Washington, D.C. (on the corner of 1st and Independence, next to the Supreme Court). Contact: Nishelle Miles (202-555-1234). Moderated by Marguerite Kelly, "Family Almanac" columnist for the *Washington Post:* 202-555-1234.

10/11 7:45 A.M.

Craig picks up Dr. Hancock at his home and drives him to the Willard Hotel (address above).

10/11 8:30 A.M.

Photo shoot at the Willard Hotel for *U.S. News & World Report* article. Dr. Walters and Aria will meet Dr. Hancock and Dave in the lobby. Contact: Alex Bowers (202-555-1234).

10/11 9:00 a.m–10:00 A.M.

In-person interview at the Willard Hotel for *U.S. News and World Report* article. Contact: Katy Kelly (202-555-1234).

10/11 11:00 A.M.–12:00 P.M.

In-studio interview (live) on NPR's *Diane Rehm Show.* Arrive at 10:45 A.M. Contact: Elizabeth Terry (202-555-1234). Address: 4000 Brandywine Street NW, Washington, D.C.

10/11 12:00 P.M.

Leave for Washington Reagan (a.k.a. National) airport for flight to

NYC. Upon arrival, take cab to Plaza Hotel (Fifth Avenue at 59th Street; 212-555-1234).

New York City

10/12 8:00 A.M.
Carey Limousine (212-555-1234) pick-up at the Plaza. Will bring you to the *Today Show* studio (30 Rockefeller Plaza, Studio 3B).

10/12 8:20 (arrival)
Today Show, in-studio interview (live). You'll go on air between 9:00 A.M. and 9:30 A.M. You have two contacts at the *Today Show*: segment producer Patricia Luchsinger (212-555-1234) and books producer Andrea Smith (212-555-1234). In a pinch, Andrea's assistant is Susan Sosnicky (212-555-1234).

10/12 9:45 A.M.
Carey Limousine to La Guardia airport for flights home.

Einstein's Error
Tour Itinerary for Dr. Allen Ranson

Emergency Numbers for Aria Johansen (Publicist)
  Work: (212) 555-1234
  Cell: (917) 555-1234
  Home: (212) 555-5678

Please see separate travel itinerary for flight information.

Note: Any gaps in this schedule may be filled by stock signings at local bookstores, to be coordinated by the author escorts.

1/25 Fly from Cleveland to NYC. Take cab to Park South Hotel (at Park and 28th), 212-555-1234.

New York City

1/26 media coaching with Biomentary, 1–4 P.M. EST, contacts: Melissa Hellen (978-555-1234 cell) and Bill McGowan (914-555-1234 office), meet them in the lobby of the Fox TV building (1211 Avenue of the Americas—48th and Sixth).

1/26 6:00 dinner with Aria at Blue Smoke; meet in hotel lobby and walk over

1/27 *Chronicle of Higher Education*, Rich Monastersky (202-555-1234). Rich to shadow all day for a "day in the life" piece. He'll call up to room from the lobby of the Park South Hotel at 10:15 A.M.

1/27 *Time Out New York*, interview by phone with reporter Barbara Spindel (305-555-1234). 10:30 A.M. EST. She'll initiate call to hotel room. Article will run in 2/13 issue.

1/27 11:00–2:00 lunch and interview with Rich (*Chronicle of Higher Education*)

1/27 2:30 arrive at the Hayden Planetarium for tech check, Central Park West at 79th; contact: Stephanie Parello (212-555-1234). Enter at the 81st Street Rose Center entrance. Upon arrival, dial Stephanie at x1234 using one of the wall phones. If she doesn't pick up, dial Elizabeth at x5678. The tech check should be completed by 3:30.

1/27 5:00 dinner with Hayden staff at local restaurant

1/27 7:00 walk back to Planetarium

1/27 HAYDEN PLANETARIUM EVENT, 7:30 p.m event in space

theater (referred to as "the dome") begins—5 minute News and Comment period, 45–50 minute lecture, 10–minute Q&A, book signing

1/28 USA Radio, *Daybreak USA*, live interview by phone, 9:00 A.M. EST, 10 minutes, Danny Miles (972-555-1234 x1234 office; 800-555-1234 x1234 studio). Danny to initiate call to hotel room.

1/28 *Newsweek*, meeting with science reporter Fred Guterl (212-555-1234), 10:00 A.M. at the *Newsweek* offices (251 West 57th)

Princeton

1/28 Take train to Princeton. Hotel: Nassau Inn, 10 Palmer Square (609-555-1234) 1/28 PRINCETON EVENT, Princeton University Store, 36 University Place, 7:00 P.M. Contact: Tracy Harkins (609-555-1234). Arrive at 6:30 P.M. to do lecture/Q&A/book signing.

1/29 Car service to Newark: A1 Limo, pick-up: 6:00 A.M., 609-555-1234.

Boston

1/29 Flight from Newark to Boston. Hotel: Marriott Cambridge, 2 Cambridge Center (617-555-1234)

1/29 *Newsweek* photo shoot in hotel room, photo editor is Annik: 212-555-1234, photographer is Melanie Dinay: 917-555-1234.

1/29 WBUR Radio (NPR, Boston), *On Point*, (nationally syndicated), 3:00, in-studio, 890 Commonwealth Avenue on the campus of Boston University, taping you reading passage from the book: "Little did Einstein know . . ." (pg 183) all the way to " . . . and that would be his legacy." (pg 184), Meghna Chakrabarti: 617-555-1234, air date tk.

1/29 HARVARD BOOKSTORE EVENT (Sackler Auditorium, 485

Broadway in Cambridge), 6-7 P.M. EST (immediately followed by reception at the Sackler—open to public—hosted by *Seed* magazine). Please arrive at 5:30 P.M. Harvard Bookstore contact is Nancy Fish: 617-555-1234. This will be a talk/Q&A/book signing. Andrew Lawler of *Science* magazine plans to attend your talk and is inviting his friend Vivian Marx (a freelance science writer). A photographer from the *Chronicle of Higher Education* will also attend and will take photos to illustrate Rich Monastersky's article.

Ann Arbor

1/30 Flight from Boston to Detroit. Hotel: Marriott Ann Arbor, 1275 S. Huron St., Ypsilanti (734-555-1234) Author escort Judy Brenneman (cell 313-555-1234) will be waiting at the bottom of the airport escalator, holding a copy of your book. She'll drive you to your radio interview and will get you to and from your event that evening.

1/30 NPR's *Todd Mundt Show*, (nationally syndicated), taped, in-studio (500 South State Street, 5000 LSA building on U. of Michigan campus in Ann Arbor), 12:15 P.M. EST, Amanda Greg (734-555-1234)

1/30 BORDERS EVENT, 7:00 P.M. EST, 612 East Liberty Street (downtown store). Meagan Kucaj (734-555-1234). Please arrive at 6:30 P.M. for this talk/Q&A/book signing.

1/31 Car service to airport: MetroCar (734-555-1234). Pick-up at 8:00 A.M.

Washington D.C.

1/31 Flight from Detroit to D.C. (Dulles). Hotel: Capital Hilton, 1001 16th Street NW (202-555-1234). Please take cab to hotel.

2/1 free day (have fun and rest up!)

2/2 WEBR Radio, "Focal Point," 4:00 P.M., in-studio (2929 Eskridge Road, Suite S, Fairfax, VA), host: Mimi Geerges (703-555-1234 studio). Please take cab to and from this interview.

2/3 WICN Radio (Worcester, MA), Inquiry, 9:30-10 A.M. EST, phoner, Mark Lynch (508-555-1234 station). Mark to initiate call to hotel room.

2/3 Powernomics Radio, Tom Pope Show, 11:15-11:30 A.M. EST, phoner, Gwen Pope (202-555-1234 x123). Gwen to initiate call to hotel room.

2/3 noon, meet author escort Paul Peachy (202-555-1234) in lobby of hotel. Visit local bookstores to sign stock on way to radio interview.

2/3 MetroNetworks Radio, Eye on Books, (nationally syndicated), taped, in-studio (8403 Colesville Rd., Suite 1500, Silver Spring, MD), 2:00-2:30 P.M. EST, host: Bill Thompson (301-555-1234).

2/3 C-Span, BookTV, 4:00 taping with Bethanne Kelly Patrick (202-555-1234 cell), in café at Olsson's Books and Records (the store at 7th and Lansbrook; 202-555-1234), will air as a half-hour interview on 2/8.

2/3 SMITHSONIAN EVENT, 7:00 pm, Ring Auditorium at the Hirshhorn Museum. Entrance is on 7th and Independence Ave. SW. Contact: Cheryl Taylor (202-555-1234). Please arrive at 6:00 P.M. for a tech check. You will be met in the lobby of the Hirshorn Museum by Cheryl or Robert Vega. This will be a 50-60 minute talk followed by 20-minute Q&A and book signing. C-Span is taping this event for Book TV (nationally syndicated).

San Francisco

2/4 Flight from D.C. (Dulles) to San Francisco. Hotel: Kimpton-Prescott Hotel, 545 Post Street (415-555-1234). Please take cab to hotel.

2/5 KZYX Radio (Ukiah, CA; Mendocino County Public Broadcasting), "Radio Curious," phoner, host: Barry Vogel (707-555-1234 studio), 8:30–9:10 A.M. PST, taped. Barry to initiate call to hotel room.

2/5 10:00 meet author escort Ellen Fishman (415-555-1234 cell) in lobby of hotel. Head over to KQED Radio studio.

2/5 KVON Radio (Napa, CA), phoner, 10:30–11:00 A.M. PST, Jeff Schechtman (707-555-1234 x123; 888-555-1234 studio). This interview will be done from KQED. Please initiate call to studio number at 10:25.

2/5 NPR's *Tech Nation*, 11:15 A.M. PST, taped, host: Moira Gunn (415-555-1234), in-studio at KQED: 2601 Mariposa in San Francisco.

2/5 KUSF Radio, in-studio (Phelan Hall in the center of the U. of San Francisco campus), host: David Reffkin (415-555-1234 studio; 415-555-1234 office), 12:30 P.M. PST

2/5 CODY'S EVENT, 7:30 P.M. (2454 Telegraph Avenue in Berkeley), Melissa Mytinger (510-555-1234). Please arrive at 7:00 P.M. for this talk/Q&A/book signing.

Seattle

2/6 Flight from San Francisco to Seattle. Hotel: Hilton Seattle, 6th and University (206-555-1234). Author escort from Joy Delf Media (206-555-1234) will meet you in baggage claim. Escort will be holding a copy of your book.

2/6 MSNBC.com, "Cosmic Log" weblog, Alan Boyle (425-555-1234), in-person interview, 3:00 at his office (One Microsoft Way, Building 25/N2, Room 2105, in Redmond)

2/6 UNIVERSITY BOOKSTORE EVENT on the University of Washington Campus, 7:00 P.M., Kane Hall, Room 220. Kim Ricketts (206-555-1234 x123). Please arrive at 6:30 P.M. for this talk/Q&A/book signing.

2/7 KMPS Radio, Introspect, 9:15 A.M. PST, in-studio (113 Dexter Avenue North, #100, Seattle), taped, Don Riggs (206-555-1234 x123). Please take a cab to this interview and then take cab to the airport.

Portland

2/7 Flight from Seattle to Portland. Hotel: Hilton Portland, 921 SW 6th Avenue Portland (503-555-1234). Please take cab to hotel.

2/7 POWELL'S EVENT (at their main store: 1005 W. Burnside), 7:30 P.M. Michal Drannen (503-555-1234). Please arrive at 7:00 P.M. PST for this talk/Q&A/book signing. Please take cab to and from this event.

2/8 Oregon Public Broadcasting (radio), "Profiles," 11–noon PST, live, in-studio (7140 SW Macadam Avenue, Portland), Dan Davis (503-555-1234), arrive 10:45 A.M. PST. Please take cab to this interview and then take cab to the airport for flight back to Cleveland.

Index

Acknowledgments

This business is something you learn by osmosis. Hang around the right people long enough and you'll know what you should do. I'd like to thank those publishing professionals from whom I've learned the most: John Radziewicz, David Goehring, Elizabeth Carduff, Matty Goldberg, Carolyn Savarese, and David Godine. I'd also like to thank four talented, tireless, and unceasingly supportive people who've worked in my department: Donna MacLetchie, Leigh Weiner, Kate Kazeniac, and Sean Maher.

Thanks to Perseus Books Group editors Amanda Cook, Marnie Cochran, and Merloyd Lawrence for giving me books I can do great things with, and for your encouragement on this project. Thanks to Susan Rabiner for helping me get my proposal in shape, and to Peter Rubie for placing it. You are two of the finest agents I know and I'm lucky to have found you. Thanks to my friend and colleague Beth Ineson who had the adjacent office at Houghton Mifflin and remains as dependable as any next door neighbor. And thanks to Gene Taft of Public Affairs who never fails to amuse. A special thank you to my editor, Philip Turner, for his faith that this was a book, and Associate Editor Keith Wallman for all his astute corrections.

Over the course of my career I've had the privilege to handle a number of wonderful authors. Only now do I see what it means to allow another to speak for your work. Berry Brazelton, Joshua Sparrow, Sandra Steingraber, Steven Wise, Howard Rheingold, Barbara Freese, Chris Locke, David Weinberger, Deborah Blum, Rudy Tanzi, Sharman Apt Russell, Jack Repcheck, Richard Meltzer, Deborah Roffman, Anne Colamosca, Bill Wolman, Justin Martin, Dan Shaughnessy—thanks for all your faith in me.

My love and thanks to Marc, who gets me.

But my biggest debt, without a doubt, is to my mother and father. From the time I was born they set about instilling a love of words, Mom never too tired to read *Bedtime for Frances* or *Chester the Worldly Pig*, Dad shouting out crossword clues in search of *le mot juste*. They supported me on a daily basis while I wrote this book—bringing cups of tea with plenty of sugar just the way I like it, picking up my dry cleaning, helping me do my taxes, filling my car with gas—always aware that holding down a full-time job while writing a book is tough, but never questioning my ability to do it. Well look you guys, we did it.

About the Author

Lissa Warren has worked in the publicity department of several prestigious Boston publishing houses including David R. Godine, Houghton Mifflin, and Perseus Publishing, and is currently Senior Director of Publicity at Da Capo Press, a member of the Perseus Books Group. She has publicized books by such authors as economist John Kenneth Galbraith, pediatrician Dr. T. Berry Brazelton, child psychiatrist Dr. Stanley Greenspan, breast cancer surgeon Dr. Susan Love, poet Mary Oliver, technology-and-culture guru Howard Rheingold, and *Boston Globe* sports columnist Dan Shaughnessy. She is an experienced promoter of both fiction and nonfiction, with particular expertise in the areas of business and biography, health and history, poetry and parenting, sports and science, and music. She has worked on such national bestsellers as *The Cluetrain Manifesto*, *Greenspan: The Man Behind Money*, *Flatterland*, *Smart Mobs*, *Faster Than the Speed of Light*, and *Touchpoints Three to Six*.

Ms. Warren holds a B.S. in English Education from Miami University and an M.F.A. in Creative Writing from Bennington College. Her poetry has appeared in such publications as *Quarterly West*, *Oxford Review*, *Black Warrior Review*, and *Verse*, and she's frequently quoted by such industry publications as *Publishers Weekly*, *Bookselling This Week*, *P.R. Week*, and *Book Publishing Report*. She has spoken about publicity at the Virginia Festival of the Book, and for Publisher's Marketing Association and the New Hampshire Writer's Project. In the fall of 2003 she taught a graduate course in book publicity at Emerson College. Ms. Warren works in Cambridge, Massachusetts, and lives on an old apple orchard in Salem, New Hampshire.